Susan,
Thank you for
your support and
your continual kindness
as you've always welcomed
me at Semily eve
and vacations. I'm to
appreciative of it and
forward to the next time a
you enjoy! Best wish

Victory's Fate

Orlando Ricci

Thank you,
Orlando Ricci

COMING SOON

Diary of a Dying Man

Published by BookLocker.com, Inc., Bradenton, Florida.

Printed on acid-free paper.

BookLocker.com, Inc.
2016

First Edition

Visit the author at:
www.imdb.me/orlandoricci
www.twitter.com/Orlando_Ricci
www.facebook.com/OrlandoJRicci
www.instagram.com/Orlando_Ricci

ACKNOWLEDGEMENTS

I want to first and foremost thank my family, friends, teammates, coaches, and former athletes for being such a significant part of my life as well as my wrestling career. Each of you has afforded me with incredible experiences that made my career and my life a positive one. I'd also like to thank West Virginia University for having been a major influence on me both academically and athletically. The five years that I spent in Morgantown, WV are some of the most memorable moments in my life and have truly formed who I am today. My time spent at WVU gave me many of the skills that aided in my ability to write "Victory's Fate" as well as become a better athlete and coach.

I'm honored to have been a member of the WVU wrestling team for five years as I formed lifelong bonds and friendships with my teammates. I loved all of my experiences at West Virginia University as a student and as an athlete and I would highly recommend that others look into joining the Mountaineer family.

I especially want to acknowledge and thank my family for everything they've done for me throughout my life as they've truly been the backbone to my success. I want to thank my brother, Gary, for having been such an important part of my life and having unconditionally supported me throughout all of my endeavors. You have been the best brother a guy could ask for, and I'm grateful for everything that you've done for me. I also want to thank my mother for being there for me and showing me the value of hard work, as she did whatever was necessary to support us, for guiding me down the right path, and affording me an opportunity to experience so much in my life. Mom, you've been an inspiration to me and I'm extremely thankful for all of the sacrifices that you've made so that I could be where I'm at today. You truly are a blessing and I love you.

I also want to thank God for giving me the skills and the ability to write this novel along with the talent and experiences as an athlete. It's been a tough road, considering it has taken over 10 years to complete this novel, but a road that I'm proud to have traveled on. At times, life has gotten in the way, but I was fortunate enough to be able to refocus myself in order to complete my first of what I hope to be many novels.

Wrestling became an important part of my life in middle school. Within a few minutes of the first day of practice, I was hooked. I knew that I had to learn everything I could about this amazing sport. I continued my career in high school where I was fortunate enough to experience success, which only solidified my desire to wrestle in college. I may not have achieved everything that I wanted to in high school or college, but I learned valuable skills and insights that I knew would aid in my future. Once I graduated from WVU, I became a coach so that I could inspire and challenge others while assisting them in gaining those same life skills and lessons that I obtained.

I was inspired to write this because of how much wrestling has meant to me throughout the more than 20 years I've been involved with it in one capacity or another. I gained so much from my years as an athlete, coach, and an official that I wanted to give back to the sport in any way possible. Wrestling gave me the drive, determination, and dedication to push myself to new heights in all aspects of my life. It taught me that hard work can lead to success and that nothing is given to you as it must be earned. I also gained an understanding on how valuable a loss can be as it's an amazing learning tool; since not everything in life goes as we plan. However, we can learn to refocus our energy and take the positives from any situation. We may not achieve all of our dreams, but everything happens for a reason. I learned that just because one goal wasn't obtained, doesn't mean that we should give up. Instead, we need to take advantage of the lessons that we've learned from our journey to become better people and athletes.

All of which contributed to me writing this novel as a tribute to everything that the sport of wrestling has given me. I just hope that I've touched the lives of my athletes as my coaches have done for me throughout my athletic career.

Few moments in life define the individual. Some are positive and some are negative. What you do with those moments make you who you are and who you will be for the rest of your life. You can either lie down and let the negatives destroy you or you can stand up and fight for what you want.

Chapter One

2014 North Carolina Wrestling State Championships

Saturday: February 22, 2014

Deep below the roaring crowd of the capacity filled Greensboro Coliseum stood Anthony Williams; an athlete who possessed an unquenchable thirst for success. He awaited his opportunity to reach the pinnacle of his career, a North Carolina High School Wrestling State Championship. The 5'9" and 152 pound junior at Parkside High School was just a few weeks shy of his seventeenth birthday. Anthony possessed a chiseled physique to go along with his mixed ethnicity, which only added to his handsome features, making him desirable to many females that he came in contact with. But he wasn't all looks, as he was also one of the brightest students at his high school and an overall good kid, who had learned many valuable lessons on respect, responsibility, and how to treat others from his parents and his coach.

Anthony Williams proudly represented Parkside High School, a large school located in Charlotte, North Carolina. Parkside was known for its diverse population of students who came there from different sections of the city and its outskirts. Some of the most influential families sent their children to Parkside, while other students came from a lower socio-economic environment. This provided Parkside with a unique intertwining of cultures and ideas, but one that worked extremely well, as the school was recognized for its academics and its production of elite athletes.

Anthony was joined by his coach, Vincent Tanzino, who was in his third season at the helm of the Parkside Mustangs. Vincent was originally from New York and descended from an Italian-American family, which led to his short and stocky stature. Vincent was only 5'7" and weighed around 180 pounds, but he was extremely well built for being in his mid-twenties. He lifted weights and worked out regularly, which helped keep his muscle mass from his days as a college wrestler at West Virginia University. He had dark black hair, with deep brown eyes and an olive complexion.

Vincent was one of the younger and more attractive teachers. He was beloved at Parkside High School, where he had taught and coached ever since he graduated from college. The students and the athletes respected his hard-nosed northern ways, as they knew that he truly had their best interests in mind. His dedication and determination was unmatched as he provided everyone with real life lessons that he intertwined with his lectures and his practices.

Vincent's continuous efforts throughout his first three seasons had built the program into a powerhouse. He did so through the use of hard work and an unparalleled dedication to the success of the team and its' athletes. Vincent would do anything he could to help his wrestlers on and off of the mat, as he not only taught them how to wrestle, but he always preached the importance of getting an education. He knew how difficult life could be, but he wanted to give those he came in contact with every possible advantage for success.

Vincent used motivational techniques to inspire those he came in contact with, and taught them that tough times are just the challenges that we go through in order to find out who we are and what we're made of. He used various quotes and philosophies to educate and to motivate his students and athletes to be strong as well as to never give up, no matter how difficult of a situation they were facing. Ultimately his goal was to provide as many of his athletes with the ability to compete at the next level and to do so on an athletic scholarship. He felt that by following his program, his athletes would truly have an opportunity for a better life.

All of which led to this moment, an opportunity for Anthony to wrestle to become a state champion and a chance for Vincent to coach one. As the exuberant crowd cheered on the competitors currently on the mat above, Anthony and Vincent were getting mentally and physically prepared for the upcoming bout. They were in an area that was specifically set up for athletes to complete their warm-ups prior to stepping foot on the mat in front of the capacity crowd that awaited them. It had two sections of a mat so that the athletes could do whatever they deemed necessary prior to their match, along with a few chairs and a public address system, allowing the competitors to hear their names being called. Anthony was filled with excitement as he anticipated his opportunity to wrestle the most important match of his young career.

Anthony was in the middle of warming up which consisted of shadow wrestling while taking this time to visualize the upcoming bout, a technique that he had grown accustom to doing and had worked extremely well for him. Anthony had a hard sweat going underneath his warm-ups, which covered his championship singlet that was specially made for a match just like this one. The singlet was bright white, with the word 'Mustangs' written in block letters down the back in Carolina blue, along with the picture of a silver Mustang with a black outline located on the left leg. It was only to be worn when one of the Parkside wrestlers made it to a finals match of a tournament, which occurred regularly for the team these days.

Once Coach Tanzino felt as though Anthony was properly warmed up, he approached him and took the opportunity to go over some last minute instructions, while encouraging his star athlete, "Remember, this is your match to take. Always set up your shots, and work for your second and third attempts if the first one doesn't work. Continue to be active and capitalize on his actions. Set the pace of the match because he won't be able to keep up with you. The match is yours for the taking!" Vincent encouragingly added, "You have more desire and talent at your age than I did, so make use of what God has blessed you with. And always remember, you won't fail!"

"I will Coach! I won't let you or my parents down," replied Anthony with a sense of determination and knowledge that he'd be victorious.

They both understood that if an athlete went into a match thinking they'd lose, then they probably would. Which is why Coach Tanzino preached how important the mind was and that the right amount of confidence, not arrogance, in one's abilities was a must.

Vincent was convinced that Anthony would win as he was by far the most talented athlete that he'd ever come across. Confidently,

Coach Tanzino replied, "I know you won't, you're too good not to! And I believe in you!"

A smile formed across Anthony's face as he was honored to be receiving such high praise from the man that he looked up to and had learned so much from. "Thanks Coach," replied Anthony. But he quickly switched his smile to a stoic look, filled with determination, focus, and an utmost desire to demolish his competition and earn the title that he had dedicated so much of his time to achieving.

At that moment the loud speaker announced, "And in the 152 pound weight class, a clash of titans. A matchup of two undefeated wrestlers as junior Anthony Williams at 41-0 takes on junior Jamie Wright at 38-0."

This prompted both wrestlers and their coaches to make their way out of the warm-up area, through the tunnel, and into the deafening arena. As they entered the arena and made their way towards the championship mat, the television announcers began discussing the upcoming bout, "These two wrestlers took similar paths throughout competition this season, having beaten everyone in their way. It's a shame that only one of them can come away as an undefeated state champion. Both were champions of their respective conferences, counties, and regionals this season. Yet, the favorite has to be Anthony Williams who is making his third trip to the state tournament; placing fifth as a freshman and third as a sophomore. He's coached by Vincent Tanzino, a former college wrestler at West Virginia University. After a successful collegiate career, he has had nothing but great fortunes in the realm of coaching. Coach Tanzino has done nearly everything except coach a state champion, but that drought might end tonight."

As the announcers finished introducing the competitors, both wrestlers and their coaches reached the center mat, which was where the battle was about to ensue. Jamie appeared nervous, while Anthony seemed anxious to get this bout underway, but confident in his ability to win. Both wrestlers finished getting ready by taking off their warm-ups, strapping up their headgear, and walking to the center of the mat to place their designated colored ankle band on their ankle and await the officials whistle. Anthony grabbed the green anklet and placed it on his right ankle, while Jamie grabbed the red one that matched his singlet and did the same. The ankle bands helped the official indicate which competitor had earned points, so that the scorers could keep an accurate point total.

As Anthony placed himself in the center of the mat, he was filled with an overwhelming sense of peace and calm, almost as if it was already in the stars for him to win this match. Just like he had played this exact moment over and over again in his head a thousand times, envisioning having his hand raised by the official, hugging Coach Tanzino and then his parents, who he imagined were overcome with joy as they smiled from ear to ear, completely proud of his accomplishment. Over the roaring crowd, he heard Coach Tanzino's final words, "This is your match to take. Set the pace and victory will be yours."

Once Jamie joined Anthony in the middle of the mat, the referee had them shake hands. Once this final pre-match task was completed, the referee immediately blew his whistle and both athletes began wrestling the other.

Anthony quickly attacked Jamie's head and worked towards gaining inside control. He maneuvered to have his right forearm placed squarely against Jamie's left clavicle, while Anthony's hand was locked firmly in place on the back of Jamie's neck. Anthony forced a substantial amount of pressure against his opponents' head, while maneuvering his left hand to obtain an inside position, by placing it on Jamie's shoulder, and gaining the ability to completely control his opponents' upper body.

Once Anthony was in position, he took a high crotch shot, but Jamie countered the move by quickly sprawling and re-shooting a single leg shot. The momentum of Jamie's shot sent both athletes out of the circle and out of bounds. The referee blew his whistle to stop the action, causing both competitors to quickly make their way back to the center of the mat.

Once they were both set, the referee blew his whistle to get the bout started again. Anthony continued to control the pace of the match as he began hand fighting, something he had grown dominant with, because Coach Tanzino placed it of the utmost importance.

Anthony immediately grabbed a Russian tie, popped Jamie's right arm up into the air, opening up his legs, and quickly took a deep double leg shot. This time he was successful, earning two points for the takedown and a 2-0 lead. Jamie immediately recovered by bellying out, as he threw his stomach to the mat to prevent giving up any more points.

As Jamie maneuvered to have his hips facing the mat, Anthony wrapped his left leg around the inside of Jamie's left leg as he began to ride legs on his opponent, a position that he loved to be in and used as a means to control his competition; a skill that would undoubtedly assist him in his collegiate career. In-spite of his dominant position and repeated attempts to earn back points, Anthony was unsuccessful in adding to his lead in the first period, leaving the score at 2-0 in his favor.

The referee flipped his coin, which landed on the mat with the green side up. Since Anthony was designated as the green wrestler, he earned the option of top, bottom, neutral, or to defer his choice to the third period. Anthony looked at Coach Tanzino who waved his hands in front of him indicating for Anthony to defer the choice to Jamie, which would allow him to choose what he wanted in the third period. This was nothing unusual, as Coach Tanzino generally preferred to have the final choice in a match.

Once the referee gave Jamie the choice, he immediately indicated that he wanted to be in the down position to start the second period. Jamie made his way to the center of the mat and set himself up in the bottom position, placing his knees and hands in back of and in front of the rectangle that was located in the center circle.

Once the official knew that Jamie was set, he told Anthony to get on top, prompting Anthony to move to Jamie's right side, placing his left hand on Jamie's stomach and his right hand on Jamie's right elbow. The referee made sure everyone was properly set before blowing his whistle to initiate the action in the second period.

Jamie tried to hit a stand-up, but as he attempted to lift his right leg up off of the mat, he was prevented by Anthony's counter of a tight waist and ankle. Anthony's action broke Jamie down, causing him to be flat on the mat. Jamie repeatedly attempted to get back to his base, but Anthony's constant forward pressure continuously broke him flat, while he tried on several occasions to turn Jamie to his back. However, neither was successful at accomplishing their moves as half of the period had already evaporated.

After numerous attempts, Jamie used every ounce of strength he could muster up as he finally returned to his base before emanating a burst of energy and speed as he successfully kicked his left leg out from underneath him, thrusting his body outwards and sinking his left hand underneath Anthony's left leg, before using his positioning to pull his body behind Anthony. The sit out to a switch that Jamie just hit, earned him two points for a reversal and knotting the score at two apiece. Jamie was now on top, doing his best to turn Anthony towards his back to earn back points and the lead; yet, he was unable to do so, as Anthony countered each of Jamie's attempts.

Both wrestlers continued to attempt various moves intended to take control of the match. Anthony cleared some space between him and his opponent as he set up and then attempted to execute a Granby Roll, but Jamie was able to counter the move by following along with a Granby of his own. This action placed Jamie in a crab riding position, causing both athletes to be sitting on their butts, while Anthony was cradled in-between Jamie's legs. On several occasions, Jamie tried to throw a leg in and earn a dominant position, but Anthony stayed tight, by keeping his arms close to his body and pulling Jamie's legs out from in-between his after each attempt, which prevented Jamie from gaining an advantage. As the seconds ticked away, neither wrestler was able to earn any points; leaving the score tied at 2-2.

It was now Anthony's choice in the third period. He looked at Coach Tanzino who pointed down, indicating that he wanted Anthony to choose the bottom position, because this gave Anthony the best chance at earning points and the lead. Once both wrestlers were set, the referee blew his whistle to start the third and final period, but was forced to immediately blow his whistle again. He put his left arm up in the air and made what looked like a 'C' with his hand. This told everyone that Jamie had moved prior to the whistle and earned himself a caution.

Anthony knew that this might give him a slight edge because Jamie likely wouldn't move as quickly this time in order to prevent getting a second caution call and become one step closer to giving Anthony a penalty point. After they had gotten reset, the referee blew his whistle once again, prompting Anthony to shoot up like a projectile out of a cannon. He got to his feet and separated his body from Jamie's before turning so that they were now standing face to face. This explosion earned Anthony one point for an escape and the lead again at 3-2 with 1:55 left on the clock in the third period.

Anthony knew that he was about to accomplish his dream of winning a state title, but he had to close out the third period before the victory would be his. Both athletes continued to work towards setting up their shots and earning a takedown, but the time seemed to be against Jamie as the clock rapidly dissipated. With 30 seconds left, Anthony felt as though he was in the perfect position as he took a single leg shot, but Jamie's hard sprawl prevented the takedown. Instead of having earned any points, Anthony was now flat on the mat with outstretched arms as he was forced to do whatever he could to hold onto Jamie's left leg. The roar of the crowd grew, barely allowing either wrestler to hear their respective coaches, who were only feet away from them, and yelling out instructions.

Coach Tanzino kept yelling for Anthony to keep a tight grip and to suck the leg up to his chest. While Jamie's coach instructed him to break Anthony's grip and spin behind to earn a takedown and the victory.

The tension was extremely high as both wrestlers tried to comply with their coaches' wishes. As Jamie pushed down on Anthony's head and tried ripping his fingers apart, Anthony's grip began to loosen up. He tried his best to hold on, but his fingers began to slip from the pressure being placed against them and the sweat that had accumulated throughout the bout; eventually causing them to separate. The seconds ticked away as Jamie tried to spin behind, but Anthony drove his left arm up into the air preventing his opponent from moving behind him. Jamie quickly pounded on Anthony's head and began to spin the other way. This time, Anthony threw up his right arm to grab Jamie's leg, but the only thing he grabbed was air as

Jamie was already past that point and had successfully spun behind. The referee threw up his left arm and held up two fingers indicating that Jamie had earned two points for the takedown.

The clock read three, two, one and the horn sounded letting everyone know that the period and the match had ended, giving Jamie Wright the victory over Anthony Williams by the final score of 4-3. Jamie immediately jumped up in jubilation as he just won what both badly coveted; the state title. Anthony slowly got up, as he was understandably upset that a poor attempt at a takedown had caused him to lose the match; a haunting mistake that he'd inevitably play over in his head countless times for the rest of his life or at least until he exacted revenge.

Anthony made his way to the center of the mat so that he could show good sportsmanship by shaking hands. After the handshake, the referee raised Jamie's arm as they turned in a complete circle, facing each member of the crowd, and indicating that he had won the 2014 North Carolina State Championship at 152 pounds to all of the fans in the arena. Cheers were heard by the capacity crowd as they had just watched two gladiators battle in an exhilarating match.

As the official let go of Jamie's arm, he ran over to his coach, exuberantly jumping into his arms, while Anthony slowly walked over to Coach Tanzino, who gave him a warm embrace. Coach Tanzino knew how hard Anthony had worked and how disappointed he must be feeling, but Vincent wanted to let Anthony know just how proud he was of his effort, while easing his pain. "Anthony, you fought hard, I'm proud of you. You had a great season, and you still have one more left."

With a hint of dejection, Anthony responded, "I know Coach T., but I wanted to get this state title badly for all of the sacrifices that you and my parents have made for me."

Vincent knew how difficult this was for Anthony, but he wanted to encourage an athlete who had become family to him, "There were no sacrifices made. We all love you and want nothing more than the best for you. I know that your parents are happy to do anything they can and are always proud of your accomplishments on and off the mat. You continue to improve and become one of the best high school wrestlers in the nation. Just think of everything that you've accomplished. You've only been wrestling for three years and you've already been to the state tournament three times. Most wrestlers would love to have accomplished all of that. Don't look at this as a negative, but as a chance for you to learn and to refocus for the bright future you have ahead of you."

This made Anthony feel a little better, "Thanks T. I know we'll get everyone next year, but I need to start by beating everyone this off-season." Anthony was determined to never have this feeling again. To never know what it was like to miss a golden opportunity at achieving his ultimate goal.

"That's the right attitude!" exclaimed Vincent. "We'll take a day or two off and get ready for the off-season tournaments and wrestling camps this summer."

"I don't need any time off," retorted Anthony, "I'm ready to begin training as soon as possible." Anthony knew that in order to achieve the success that he desired, he needed to get right back to work as he believed that time off would only make him weak.

Coach Tanzino smiled as he knew he would have felt the exact same way when he was in high school, "Okay, we'll work out tomorrow. Let's go get you to your parents and the team. I'm sure everyone wants to see you."

Anthony and Vincent made their way back into the same tunnel that only moments earlier they had walked out of with high hopes of accomplishing their goal of obtaining a state championship. They left knowing that this would be the most important off-season of Anthony's career as there was a lot of hard work to be done in order to prepare Anthony to obtain the title that had eluded him so far in his illustrious career.

Chapter Two

The Day After

Sunday: February 23, 2014

The sun was barely up and peeking through the blinds in Vincent's bedroom when his cell phone began to ring and vibrate on his nightstand. Vincent was still half asleep as he looked at the clock, which read 8:30, before reaching over and grabbing his phone.

In a groggy voice, Vincent answered, "Hello."

"T., did I wake you?" questioned Anthony.

It was taking Vincent a moment to focus on what was going on. He held one eye open, as he responded, "Yeah, its 8:30 on a Sunday morning."

"Sorry, I was already up and ready to start working out. Do you know what time you want to meet at the school? Because I'm ready whenever you are," stated Anthony with excitement in his voice.

"I was hoping to get a little sleep in this morning, especially since we didn't get back until 2 am."

"I know, but I really wanted to study some of my matches from states and regionals. Besides, I was hoping that you wanted to wrestle and lift weights, since you said that you'd be cool with working out today."

"I did say that," stated Vincent as he remembered his comments from the previous evening. "Okay, give me a half hour to get ready and over to the school and we'll get a good workout in."

"Great! Thanks T. I'll see you in a little bit."

"Bye Anthony," replied Vincent as he ended the call. He slowly and quietly got out of bed and reached for a pair of sweats that were on the floor to throw on for his drive over to Parkside High School.

Vincent tried to move quietly as to not wake up Vanessa, his girlfriend, and the love of his life, who was still asleep in bed. Vanessa and Vincent had been dating for nearly three years. The two met shortly after each had moved to town after graduating from their respective colleges. Vanessa Clarke graduated from the University of North Carolina at Chapel Hill with a Bachelor's Degree in Business. They both were former collegiate athletes and fell in love at first sight when they met at a mutual friend's party.

Vanessa was a soccer star in college, as she was the starting center mid-fielder on two national championship teams, and a huge lover of all types of sports, which was a major basis for their relationship. Her speed, agility, ball handling skills, and vision of the field made her one of the top recruits coming out of high school and aided in her success in college. Right before she graduated from UNC, Vanessa debated about trying out for the US Women's National Team, but after she was hired to be a Pharmaceutical Sales Representative for a big company in Charlotte, she decided to give up the sport that she loved in order to focus on her career.

Vanessa was 5'5" with long black hair, a dark skin tone, green eyes, with a 120 pound petite yet athletic frame, and absolutely gorgeous. Her beauty was only enhanced by her heritage as she was part Jamaican, English, and German, which allowed for a stunning blend of features. She had grown up in Fort Lauderdale, Florida, where she excelled academically and athletically, before making the move to North Carolina.

Through Vanessa's relationship and love for Vincent, she became a big supporter of his team, making it to most of their matches and tournaments. She had also grown close to Anthony and the Williams' as they had become family to Vincent.

As Vincent was quietly putting on his sweats, Vanessa's voice came from the other side of the bed, "Where are you going?"

Vincent looked over at his beautiful girlfriend and replied, "That was Anthony on the phone. He wants to workout, so I'm going to be gone for a couple of hours. Stay in bed and get some sleep. I'll be back before you know it."

Vanessa didn't even fight Vincent as this had become the norm. "Okay, have a good workout."

Vincent walked over to Vanessa's side of the bed, bent over, gave her a kiss and told her that he loved her. Vanessa gladly reciprocate his affection as she gave him a passionate kiss and told him that she loved him prior to rolling into the center of the bed and spreading out, taking over the entire bed with her tiny frame.

Vincent glanced at his beautiful girlfriend and smiled, as he thought about how lucky he was to have met someone as amazing as her. He was so happy and so in love with Vanessa. She was one of the most understanding women that he had ever met. She completely accepted him for who he was and the career path that he had chosen.

Vincent left the bedroom and walked downstairs to the kitchen to grab breakfast; a banana and a bottle of water. He didn't open them up right away as he figured he'd eat and drink on the ride over to the high school. With his breakfast in hand, Vincent proceeded to walk out the front door and make his way to his black Jeep Wrangler which was sitting in the driveway.

It usually took Vincent 15 minutes to get to work and today was no different. As he approached the school, he could see the big Carolina blue sign that had written in white letters, "Welcome to Parkside High School. Home of the Mustangs." Next to the sign was a huge statue of a Mustang that had been donated by the senior class of 1997.

The high school was opened in 1950, making it one of the oldest schools in the area, but was surprisingly in great condition even though there had only been minor repairs to the buildings throughout the years. The school had always been known for its continued production of phenomenal student-athletes as it was a perennial powerhouse in football, baseball, women's soccer, and women's track and field; however, wrestling had always lagged behind, until Vincent took over the program.

Vincent had just completed his third season as the Head Wrestling Coach, which was his best to date. He went 8-8 his first season, with two state qualifiers, both of whom took fifth place, giving the team a twenty-fifth place finish in the state tournament. His second season brought about a 16-11 record, third place in their conference, and four state qualifiers. Two of the qualifiers placed third, one took fourth, and the last took fifth, which gave the team a tenth place finish. This season took the team to new heights as they went 22-4, placed second in their conference, fifth in the state dual tournament, second place in the regional tournament, and had five state qualifiers. The team took sixth at the state championships, with a fourth place finisher, two third place finishers, and Anthony Williams leading the way with his second place finish. The team was only getting better and had a promising future under the tutelage of Coach Tanzino. The school was proud of what he had accomplished and fully supported his program.

When Vincent finally pulled around to the back of the school, where the wrestling practice room was located, he was greeted by a smiling high school wrestler. Anthony was an unbelievably bright student, who just happened to be an outstanding athlete. He used the same intensity that made him successful as an athlete in everything that he did. Anthony was beloved in the community for being an amazing person with a heart of gold. He also possessed extraordinary strength, speed, and mental fortitude giving him an edge over most other competitors.

Anthony's parents were hard working upstanding members of the community, who sacrificed whatever they could to provide a better life, than they had, for their only child. They had fallen in love in college and were married shortly afterwards, much to the dismay of both of their families. Their union led to both of them being disowned and all ties severed. Their families didn't agree with the two of them getting married because they were of different ethnic backgrounds. Terrance Williams grew up in an African-American household while Olivia Williams grew up in an Italian family. This caused Anthony to grow up without knowing his relatives and experiencing what it was like to have a large extended family. All he had were his parents, his friends, his teammates and now Coach Tanzino, who had grown to be another member of their family.

Vincent pulled up and parked his Jeep in his usual spot, the two closest parking spaces to the wrestling room. The building was built five years earlier by a former graduate and wrestler at Parkside High School in the hopes that one day the program would be made into a powerhouse, like it was currently on its way of becoming. The money was donated on the premise that the room would only be used by the wrestling team for their yearlong training. Coach Tanzino made full use of the top notch facility that he had the pleasure of working in.

The wrestling building held two practice mats, its own weight room, stair steppers, and stationary bikes along with a big locker room and office for the coaching staff. On the wall were silhouettes of wrestlers in various holds along with inspirational quotes and sayings. Trophy cases were located at the front of the room and held all of the trophies that the team had earned, most coming over the past three seasons, along with team pictures as well as player stats and records. This allowed the team to be reminded on a daily basis of the success that they've had and the goals that they wanted to achieve.

As Vincent opened his door, he was given a big hug by Anthony, "Thanks Coach for coming so early today. I just couldn't sleep anymore and I wanted to get my training started right away."

"No problem Anthony. I'm always up for a good workout."

Anthony handed Vincent a bag, "I brought you a bagel. I figured you hadn't eaten yet this morning."

Vincent smiled as he appreciated the gesture. He grabbed the bag from Anthony, "Thanks. Actually I had a banana, but I'll take the bagel anyways."

They walked over to the practice facility where Vincent unlocked the door. They entered the building and immediately headed towards Vincent's office to watch some of Anthony's matches from the previous two weekends. His office had a large desk, that was covered in papers and notes that Vincent had taken. A plush leather chair was situated behind the desk and two more sat on the opposite side for others to sit in. There was also a couch, a mini-fridge, a white board, a TV that was mounted to the wall and two filing cabinets; all of which were new and gave Vincent a comfortable place to complete his work and to study for the teams' opponents. Vincent felt lucky as he couldn't have asked for a better place to work as he recognized that most high schools didn't have anything even remotely close to this.

Inside, Coach Tanzino gave Anthony a piece of paper and told him to write down his short and long term goals. This was nothing new to Anthony because every year Coach held two meetings with each athlete so that they could set their goals for the season and then to see how those goals were progressing. Anthony quickly wrote down six items, as he had been thinking about what he wanted to accomplish all night long.

1) Train harder than everyone else and continue to improve.
2) Win both the Freestyle and Greco-Roman State Championships.
3) Earn All-American honors in Folkstyle, Freestyle, and Greco-Roman.
4) Go undefeated throughout my senior season.
5) Win States!!!
6) Earn a wrestling scholarship to the college of my choice.

Anthony then read the six goals to Coach Tanzino, who was pleased with what he heard and knew the training that was needed for him to accomplish all six of his lofty, yet reasonably attainable goals.

While Anthony was writing his goals, Vincent had gotten the video system ready to replay his matches. They began the film session with the regional championships. Anthony and Vincent both pointed out mistakes and moments when Anthony didn't fully take advantage of what errors his opponents made. They even noticed how Anthony was too predictable at times as he left himself open for counter moves. These were all situations where Anthony was susceptible and would have to work to prevent those scenarios from happening again as he might not be as lucky the next time.

Once they finished with the regional championships, they began to watch his state championship matches. They were ultimately pleased with what they had watched with all of his matches, until they made it to the finals bout, which he had just lost twelve hours earlier. Even though it was hard to watch, Anthony picked out a number of errors in judgment, especially taking an extremely poor shot with a short time left on the clock in a match he was winning. Anthony noticed how he didn't use a proper set-up; instead, he dove at Jamie's leg and blew his chance at a state title. This upset Anthony, but he needed to learn from his mistakes and move forward towards accomplishing his new goals. Which Anthony hoped would eventually lead to at least one rematch with Jamie Wright, and a chance at redemption.

After studying the various matches and discussing some of the ways in which Anthony could improve his skills and accomplish his goals, both Vincent and Anthony got ready for an intense workout. They began by going through the usual warm-up that was in place to get their heart rates up while also allowing them to stretch out their muscles. They performed the various exercises prior to getting a good stretch in.

After warming up, Vincent setup a number of stations for the two of them to go through as a part of their circuit training that they'd complete prior to starting the wrestling portion of the workout. The exercises were organized in a way that would work on all muscle groups and produce the best results possible. The object was to increase lean muscle mass while improving the athletes conditioning.

Once they were tired from going through the circuit training twice, they began to drill wrestling moves. They started with setups and shots, prior to working on top and bottom moves. They drilled for 15 minutes before completing two 10 minute live matches which caused them and the mat to be covered in sweat. A puddle had formed on the mat below each of them as they took a short break before finishing up their workout. Vincent and Anthony were both tired after wrestling, but still proceeded to complete 30 minutes on the stair steppers. This was just the beginning to what would inevitably be an intense off-season of training and competition; which both Vincent and Anthony were looking forward to. They knew how important the next few months would be for Anthony's continued development and his recruitment which they were certain would result in a full scholarship to the school of his choice.

Chapter Three

The Off-Season

March-June, 2014

The Parkside wrestlers knew what it would take to win the Mid-West Conference Championship and hopefully a North Carolina State Championship in the years to come; intense off-season training. The training consisted of a Freestyle and Greco-Roman team that was coached by Vincent Tanzino and two area head coaches, from the Lake Norman Lancers and the Mooresville Marauders, who were extremely experienced and well respected. The other coaches brought a few of their athletes with them, while a select number of local wrestlers, from various teams, were invited to join as well. This made for an extremely talented and competitive squad, almost equivalent to an All-Star Team.

A few of the Mustangs played baseball or were on the track and field team during the spring, but the rest were present and accounted for as they worked hard on the mat in order to continuously improve. Even though those athletes were participating in other sports, a number of them made a few practices and tournaments throughout the off-season so that they could remain crisp.

Each wrestler made vast improvements as they battled each other in practice twice a week and at times wrestled one another in the tournaments that they were entered in almost every weekend. They traveled to various tournaments across North Carolina and other states to constantly find the best competition possible. They made the rounds to Georgia, South Carolina, Virginia, and Florida as they found unrelenting challenges.

Vincent also hosted a tournament at Parkside High School, inviting some of the best wrestlers, and teams, from across the nation. In-spite of participating in these top notch tournaments, the team was able to perform extremely well. The success that they were enjoying enhanced their recognition as one of the elite off-season prep teams in North Carolina and in the nation.

Due to the success obtained throughout all of the off-season tournaments, many of the wrestlers were making quite a name for themselves as most of them were receiving letters from college coaches who were interested in possibly offering them an opportunity to further their wrestling careers. However, nobody was being recognized more than Anthony Williams.

While participating in the out of state events, Anthony and his teammates faced top of the line competition. In every tournament, Anthony and the others were battling against state qualifiers, state place-winners, and state champions from all over the country; many of whom were nationally ranked. These difficult matches allowed each athlete to see what they were made of as they built confidence in their skills and abilities. Ultimately, the athletes were increasing their chances of success in the upcoming season.

Along the way, Anthony was tasked with the undertaking of having to face off against formidable opponents from New York, New Jersey, Georgia, West Virginia, South Carolina, Ohio, Virginia, Florida, Illinois, Pennsylvania, and even California; which included dozens of wrestlers who were ranked in various national polls. All of whom were being highly sought after by a variety of colleges, while a few had already signed their national letter of intent, but none were able to solve the riddle of how to defeat Anthony and stop his dominance.

Sunday: April 6, 2014

Instead of cutting weight throughout the off-season and remaining in the 152 pound weight class, Anthony made the calculated move to compete at 160 pounds, which was more of a natural weight for him. Both Vincent and Anthony felt that this would be a great opportunity to allow him to get prepared for his jump to 160 during his senior year as well as either wrestling in the 157 or 165 pound weight classes in college.

In the beginning of April, Vincent and Anthony, along with his parents, traveled to Cedar Falls, Iowa in order to compete at the USA Folkstyle Nationals. The event was run by the USA Wrestling Organization, which is one of the two major governing bodies associated with off-season wrestling. The tournament was being held at the UNI-Dome and hosted an unprecedented amount of talent. It was a who's who of high school wrestlers. Due to his second place finish at the state championships, Anthony had qualified to participate in the event. Vincent only wished that he would've been able to bring more athletes from either of his teams, but he knew, that in due time, he'd have a lot more qualify to participate in such an elite tournament.

The grueling two day tournament saw numerous state champions taste defeat. For most of the wrestlers, it was unlike anything that they had ever felt before. These athletes were used to stepping on the mat as the prohibitive favorite, but this weekend was different. Most of them walked into the arena as underdogs. But for Anthony, he was fortunate enough to find a way to pull out victory after victory on his way to the championship match at 160 pounds.

Anthony wasn't alone as his nemesis Jamie Wright had also made the trip to Iowa for the tournament. However, he decided to remain in the 152 pound weight class, where he had earned his state championship. He didn't mind cutting weight for the event, as he ultimately felt that 152 gave him a better opportunity to triumph. Yet, he didn't experience as much success as Anthony.

After winning his first match of the weekend, Jamie was beaten handily in his second round bout, forcing him into the consolation brackets. Jamie was able to earn two more victories while he wrestled back, before finally being eliminated, which prevented him from placing in the top eight or earning All-American honors. It was a good performance for the junior, but not good enough to garnish very much recognition from major college programs. Jamie's results weren't nearly as impressive as Anthony's, who ended up being the lone place-winner to come out of North Carolina at the heralded event.

After two days of tough competition, Anthony found himself in the championship match against the highly recruited John Maggiano out of New York. Maggiano had just finished his senior season out of

Saint Marks High School in New York City, where he had capped off his third straight New York State Championship, and his second straight undefeated season. His last defeat, of any kind, happened as a sophomore in this same event, when he lost in the finals. To Maggiano, this was just another opportunity to showcase his dominance over anyone he wrestled against as well as defend his Folkstyle National Championship from 2013, before beginning his collegiate career in the fall at Cornell.

Anthony knew that this was going to be an arduous task, as Maggiano, along with most other wrestlers from New York, were known for being dominant on their feet. But, considering that Coach Tanzino grew up in New York himself, Anthony felt confident that he had been taught many of the same skills that his opponent possessed. Besides, he hadn't made it this far just to doubt himself or his abilities.

As the match began, both athletes showed the crowd why they were in the finals. Anthony and John showed off their hand-fighting skills as they tried on several occasions to set-up a takedown. Shot after shot, sprawl after sprawl, were completed by both competitors, neither being able to gain a strong-hold on his opponent. There were numerous flurries throughout the first period of action, but nobody was able to capitalize, causing them to remain scoreless after a hard fought two minutes of relentless action.

As the second period began, Anthony found himself on bottom. Both he and Coach Tanzino had scouted John and were aware of the fact that he was a leg rider. Anthony took this knowledge and anticipated a spiral ride to legs being thrown in. As John did just that, Anthony caught his opponent's right leg with his right arm, as it was being maneuvered into position, preventing it from being locked into place around his leg. Anthony immediately used his left hand to pull John's right leg underneath him further and out the other side, causing John's hips to slide below Anthony's. This was Anthony's chance, as he continued to pull his opponent's leg with his left hand; he used his right arm to slide up and around John's waist. As Anthony threw his hips up and into his opponent, John fell to his butt on the mat, allowing Anthony to step his legs and body around his opponents, earning him a reversal.

The official made a circular motion with both of his arms, near his chest, before holding up two fingers, indicating to the scorers and the crowd that Anthony had indeed earned two points for the reversal. With a 2-0 lead in the second, Anthony pressed the action as he attempted a variety of moves intended to turn his opponent to his back. But, neither wrestler gave an inch in the battle, as time ran out of the period without another point being scored.

The third period gave John his choice of a position, and without hesitation, he chose down. It only took fifteen seconds of continual motion for John to open up enough space for himself to stand-up and earn one point for an escape. It was now 2-1 in Anthony's favor, as both competitors were on their feet in the neutral position, where they both felt extremely comfortable. John instantly was on the attack and before Anthony knew it, John had already taken three solid shots, all of which Anthony was fortunate enough to defend, but was prevented from being on the offensive himself. The referee lifted his right arm in the air and called out that Anthony had just been hit with a stalling warning as he wasn't attempting any offense.

Anthony couldn't remember the last time that he had been given a stalling call, but he didn't want to get another call against him, as it would give his opponent a penalty point and tie up the match. This warning lit a match under Anthony as he instantly became aggressive. He wasn't going to just stand there and take this offensive barrage without a counter attack.

With only 45 seconds left in the period, both athletes worked on gaining an edge. Anthony took advantage of John's forward pressure, as he used his left under hook to throw John's right arm by him, opening his opponent up and allowing Anthony to grab John's right leg with his right arm. Anthony lifted his opponent's leg up into the air, quickly planting it on his right shoulder. This caused John to be off-balanced and forced him to hop on one leg to remain upright. Anthony quickly kicked out John's left leg, forcing his opponent to belly out as he fell towards the mat, with Anthony following behind, landing on top of him and in complete control.

Anthony had just earned two points for the takedown, for a 4-1 lead, which wasn't enough to satisfy him as he pressed the action, but in a controlling manner, as he didn't want to make a mistake that would cause him to lose another championship. Anthony earned a cheap tilt due to one of John's attempts to get free, and with it, three more points, opening the gap to 7-1, before riding his opponent out for the rest of the period.

As the clock struck zero, and the referee blew his whistle, Anthony let go of the stronghold that he had on his opponent. Anthony stood up, knowing that he had just won a Folkstyle National Championship, and with it, gained back some respect from anyone who doubted his abilities; especially after the heartbreaking lose he suffered at the hands of Jamie Wright just six weeks earlier.

After the official raised his hand, he quickly ran over to Coach Tanzino and gave him a big hug, before making his way to the stands to do the same with his parents. Everyone was filled with excitement, as Anthony had just achieved one of his major goals for the off-season. He was now a National Champion, a feat that most athletes were unable to achieve; no matter the sport they played.

May 9-10, 2014

On Saturday and Sunday, May 9th and 10th, the Mustang Wrestling Club participated in the 43rd Annual North Carolina Freestyle and Greco-Roman State Championships, which were being held close to home, as they only had to drive 20 minutes to the Mooresville Arena for the tournament. This event was the precursor to the National Championships in Fargo, North Dakota that were being held in July. The top two wrestlers from each weight class would be eligible to represent their state at the event in two months, and Vincent felt good about his athletes' chances at qualifying for the right to challenge the best of the best from across the nation.

Throughout Saturday, the athletes competed in the Greco-Roman portion of the competition. As the day progressed, Vincent watched as Anthony won a Junior Greco-Roman state title in the 160 pound weight class, while Ryan Thompson, one of his Parkside wrestlers, took second place at Heavyweight, in the Cadet Division. By placing in the top two, both athletes automatically qualified for their chance to compete in Fargo during the summer.

Ryan Thompson was a talented multi-sport athlete at Parkside High School. As a sophomore, he was one of five athletes to play Varsity Football as an underclassman, four of which also wrestled. The Football Coaches recognized how much wrestling helped them to become better football players and rewarded them with an opportunity to shine at the higher level. Ryan was the starting left tackle and a starting defensive lineman for the team. He also was a shot putter in the spring. At 6'3" and 270 pounds, he was a mammoth of an athlete, who used a combination of strength, speed, and agility to his advantage in all three sports. Many of the students at Parkside called him "Beast" due to his athletic prowess and size. Vincent felt good about the young man's future as he had already qualified for states that season and now for the National Championships in Fargo.

Many of the other wrestlers made valiant attempts at qualifying, but were unsuccessful. However, Vincent knew that his athletes would fare much better throughout the following day, in the Freestyle competition, which his team excelled in.

On Sunday, the Mustang Wrestling Club saw even more success as they took a commanding control of the Freestyle State Championships. The team was led by Anthony Williams, as he won a second Junior State Championship, which afforded him with the opportunity to compete in both styles in Fargo.

Matt States also qualified with a second place finish in the 100 pound weight class of the Cadet Division. Matt was the starting 106 pound wrestler for the Mustangs, and as a freshman, he had quite a bit of success, as he fell one win shy of qualifying for the State Championships. He had benefitted from being around the team for the past couple of years, as he watched his older brother, Chris, compete. He also learned how to wrestle from Chris and Anthony, who had taught him many of the basics, prior to being on the team this year. They had spent countless hours drilling moves at home or at Anthony's, making Matt a guaranteed starter for the Mustangs, and one who could win right away.

Chris States also wrestled well throughout the weekend, as he earned a Junior Freestyle State Championship at 120 pounds. Chris was one of three juniors who were going to be a part of the senior leaders of the Mustangs throughout the upcoming season. He wrestled at 120 pounds throughout his junior year where he placed fourth in the 2014 North Carolina State Championships. Since he was planning on remaining at 120 for his senior season, he wanted to wrestle that weight class throughout the off-season. Chris only stood at 5'5", but what he lacked in stature, he made up for in other ways.

They were also joined by Tim Ridley, who had taken the weekend off from his baseball schedule to compete in this event. Even though he hadn't spent much time on the mat throughout the off-season, he still was able to win a Junior State Championship. Tim decided to wrestle at 182 pounds, which was heavier than normal, as he didn't want to cut weight and hurt his ability to be a power hitter during baseball season.

Tim was normally at 170 pounds, where he had placed third at the 2014 State Wrestling Championships. In-spite of his success as a wrestler, he had high hopes of going to college to play baseball. Tim was an athlete who liked to lead by example, more so than through giving grand speeches. His work ethic led him to be named a team captain, alongside Anthony, which was voted on by his teammates. Tim was 6' tall, with blonde hair and an athletic build. He was more concerned with his athletic career than anything else, which is why he earned good grades, but nothing to brag about. Tim had the pleasure of being one of Anthony's main workout partners, but unfortunately for him, he didn't have a lot of success at beating the much more talented Anthony Williams.

Besides the Parkside Mustangs, many of the other athletes who came to Parkside High School from across Charlotte, to participate with the Mustang Wrestling Club, saw success. The team added two more Greco-Roman qualifiers, one of which was a champion, while the other was a runner-up. Along with four more Freestyle qualifiers, two of which won the tournament, while two more placed second.

In total, the highly regarded team had four Greco-Roman qualifiers to compete in Fargo at the National Championships, and eight in Freestyle, which was by-far the most for any team in the state. Vincent and the other coaches were pleased at the results, even though they felt as if a few more of their athletes could have made it. But, they took their experiences as a learning tool to be used throughout the remainder of the off-season and into the training camps that they'd be participating in. This was a major step in the evolution of Coach Tanzino's program, which appeared to have a very bright future.

After competing in the North Carolina Freestyle and Greco-Roman State Championships, the Mustang Wrestling Club finished the off-season with a few more tournaments, before making the rounds to the summer camps. All of which were scheduled to take place prior to the biggest event that they'd be involved with, the National Championships in Fargo.

In-spite of the difficult road he went down, Anthony had yet to experience defeat throughout the off-season as he was working on achieving an undefeated campaign, which already included a Folkstyle National Championship as well as a North Carolina State Championship in both Freestyle and Greco-Roman, along with qualifying for another trip to Fargo, North Dakota for a chance at two more National Championships.

Even with all of his success, Anthony couldn't stop agonizing over one thing, the unexpected defeat that he suffered in the state finals to Jamie Wright. Anthony knew that Jamie was the one person standing in his way of total dominance, perfection, and that allusive high school state championship. He just hoped that Jamie planned to move up to 160, where he intended on being during his senior season, because he wanted another chance at beating him. To Anthony, it was a way to validate everything that he had done throughout his career and make others realize that it was just a fluke that he had even lost in the first place.

All of Anthony's success had enhanced his opportunity to receive a college scholarship. Anthony's name had sky-rocketed to the top of the recruiting list at a number of colleges across the nation. Coaches were sending letters and making phone calls to both Anthony and Vincent, trying to see what university Anthony wanted to continue his wrestling career at. The Williams' family had a lot of trust in Vincent to help guide Anthony through this tough decision as they knew that Coach Tanzino always had his athletes' best interests in mind.

Besides the tournaments, Vincent was well-aware that another excellent opportunity for college coaches to recruit athletes was at summer wrestling camps. Each year the entire Parkside team traveled as a group to one team camp, which was always at West Virginia University, Coach Tanzino's alma mater, because he felt as though it was a great opportunity for his athletes.

The Parkside Mustangs had won the camp championship the previous year and were set on defending it, which they were quite successful in doing. Vincent not only brought his team, but he also worked as one of the camp technicians, showing a variety of techniques to all of the athletes present. He did this as a means to stay involved with his alma mater along with building his reputation within the wrestling community. Vincent was gaining recognition as an elite coach, and was being considered a hot commodity for various college coaching opportunities.

Many local coaches even tried to entice Vincent to work their camps, but Vincent was more concerned with providing the best possible environment for his athletes to improve their skills and afford them with an opportunity to be scouted by as many college coaches as possible. Besides, Vincent didn't want to give all of his secrets away to the teams he'd be competing against, which was another factor into why he only worked at the WVU camp, because most of the local teams didn't travel very far outside of the area.

While at the camps, Anthony was not only learning new moves or variations to the moves he already knew, but he was also gaining knowledge on how to perfect the arsenal he currently had at his fingertips. He not only wanted to demonstrate that he could do any move, but that his opponent could be aware of what was coming, yet, they still wouldn't be able to stop it. Thus, allowing him to completely dominate any competitor who stepped foot on the mat with him.

The college coaches at the camps noticed Anthony's dominance over his opponents as well as his willingness to adapt and make changes in order to improve on every aspect of his wrestling. Anthony was never satisfied with the skills that he already possessed. Instead, he had an undeniable thirst to be the best wrestler ever. Anthony continuously wanted to know more and perfect everything in his repertoire. He was well-aware of how lucky he was to have Vincent as his coach, a man who had repeatedly experienced success in his own career, and a man who wanted to teach everything that he knew to his athletes. A man who took time out of his schedule to council an athlete who needed it or traveled with his wrestlers all over the United States to provide them with skills and experiences that would inevitably bring them success and opportunities for a bright future in all aspects of their lives.

Anthony not only grew as a wrestler, but also as a leader, not just with his teammates, but with all of the other athletes that he came in contact with. His willingness to take the time to help a beginning wrestler learn the basics didn't go unnoticed by the college coaches. His leadership, drive, determination, and desire to be the most dominant wrestler in the nation, had coaches salivating at the idea of landing this top recruit. However, many of the college coaches knew that they'd have to convince Vincent that they'd treat Anthony right, because they realized that he was the key to landing this superstar.

Yet, some coaches were fearful that they didn't have a chance with Anthony, because they believed that Vincent would sway the decision towards his alma mater, but that wasn't the case. Vincent wanted nothing but the best for Anthony, no matter where he ended up. In-spite of his overwhelming desire for Anthony to follow in his footsteps, Vincent was helping him make an educated and informed decision by weighing all of the options and seeing what would be the best fit for him on the mat and in the classroom.

Anthony wanted to find the collegiate program that would provide him with a competitive environment along with top notch coaches and teammates who would push him to achieve greatness, not only on the mat, but off of it as well. He wanted an institution that would stimulate his mind, not just his body. An institution that could give him more than just a National Championship, but a degree that would last him a lifetime and provide a living for him and one day his family. A chance for Anthony to live a comfortable life, not one where he, nor his family, would have to struggle like his parents often had to in order to provide for him.

Yet, without a full-ride, he was afraid that his parents couldn't afford to pay for his education. Due to their income, he unfortunately couldn't qualify for financial aid. And even though both of his parents worked full-time jobs, they didn't make enough to pay for all of his tuition. They were too middle class to get help, so he had to rely solely on his athletic and academic accomplishments to provide for his future. Besides, Anthony knew that they had already spent all of their money on allowing him to have so many amazing opportunities, ones that they never experienced for themselves as they grew up. Anthony was cognizant of the sacrifices that his parents made to send him to all of the camps, off-season training, off-season tournaments as well as their beautiful house on the lake and he wanted to earn a scholarship as a way to repay them for all of their hard work. He truly appreciated everything that they had done for him and loved them more than any words or actions could relay.

Most of the team had been on the go since the end of the high school season, which had immediately turned into their off-season training. It hadn't left much time for anything else, but it had shown Vincent who was truly dedicated to achieving greatness. Once the Parkside Mustangs returned home from the West Virginia University Wrestling Camp, it was time for them to take a short break before making their next, and final, journey of the off-season. This provided a much needed, and well deserved, few days of rest; not only for the athletes, but for Vincent as well.

Vincent dedicated most of his free time to his team and unfortunately caused him, at times, to neglect his beautiful and understanding girlfriend, Vanessa. But he did everything in his power to make up for it when he was with her as he treated her like gold. Vanessa really didn't mind because she understood the commitment necessary to be a successful coach and athlete. Instead, Vanessa respected and loved how dedicated and driven Vincent was. She took everything in stride as she made the most of the time that they had together. She loved Vincent and would do whatever was necessary to make their relationship work.

Vincent knew that Vanessa was special. She was truly a catch, as she was not only beautiful and intelligent, but she was also kind, loving, understanding and the most amazing woman that he had ever come across. Her desire to succeed and willingness to make whatever sacrifices were needed to achieve her goals at work and with their relationship was evident to Vincent. He supported her in every way he could and made sure to communicate with her every chance that he had.

Vincent did the little things, like buying her flowers or sending her cards from the road or taking her out to nice dinners when he was around. Vincent wanted nothing more than to make this relationship work and felt blessed with the fact that Vanessa understood the importance of the impact that he was having on so many teenagers' lives. If he could've imagined the perfect woman, it would easily have been Vanessa. She had no faults in his eyes, and what some might consider faults, Vincent didn't, as he accepted those quirks as who she was and loved everything that she brought to the table. He was head over heels in love with her and he wouldn't have wanted it any other way.

Chapter Four

July Fourth Festivities

Friday: July 4th, 2014

Anthony and Vincent had only been back in town a few days, from the West Virginia University Team Camp, when the Annual Williams' Fourth of July celebration took place. The two of them, along with the other qualifiers, were scheduled to head back out of town in two weeks, after completing their third and final training camp of the summer. This meant that Anthony needed to try and have as much fun as possible while he was back in Charlotte. And Anthony couldn't think of a better way to enjoy himself than with his family and friends.

The regulars were in attendance at the Williams' residence, Terrance and Olivia Williams, Anthony and Amanda, Vincent and Vanessa, Tim, Ben, Brittany, Al, Aisha, Chris and Anthony's Boxer Sammie. Sammie had been named after Anthony's favorite wrestler of all time and over the past three years, Anthony had studied all of his footage from college, as a World Team Member and an Olympian, and loved his hard-nosed, never give up, attitude. Anthony even tried to mimic what he saw in those old matches as he hoped to have as great of a career as the legend himself.

Anthony's girlfriend Amanda Arnold was by his side the entire day long. She was a beautiful 5'6" blond, with crystal blue eyes, a wonderfully big and bright smile, and an extremely perky personality. Some might have considered her to be somewhat ditzy, but that was a misconception as she was extremely book smart; however, at times, she did lack in common sense. Amanda was a year behind Anthony as she was only going into her junior year of high school.

The two had been dating for a year and spent as much time together as possible, which unfortunately at times wasn't very much. Amanda never missed an opportunity to watch Anthony wrestle as she usually drove to away matches and tournaments with his parents or any friend who would go with her. Her love for Anthony was evident to everyone that saw the two of them together. She absolutely adored her boyfriend, as she was willing to do anything for him. Amanda was very patient and understanding about the fact that she hardly got to see Anthony because of his off-season schedule. But, whenever they did have time together, she knew that she had to take full advantage of the precious moments with him.

Tim Ridley, one of the senior leaders of the team, was also in attendance. He had grown close to the other two senior wrestlers over the past three years, as he had only lived in the area since middle school. Tim's father received a promotion with his job at a bank, causing them to leave a rural area of South Carolina, for the city life in Charlotte. His quiet demeanor didn't bring with it a lot of friendships prior to him playing sports at Parkside. But he was a loyal friend, as he'd do anything for those that he cared about.

Chris States was the final senior on the team, and the most entertaining of all of them. He took his infectious smile and his witty ways with him everywhere he went. He enjoyed life and making others laugh. He was known for being the team's prankster and the senior class clown. This might have gotten others into trouble, but Chris had a knack for talking his way out of situations. Chris was skilled at lightening the mood and having a fun time no matter what was going on around him. At times, this led to a lack of focus, but whenever Anthony got on his case to be serious, he'd heed the warning and immediately shaped up, even if it was only for a short period of time.

Ben Branson, an 18-year-old upcoming senior, was another one of the guests and one of Anthony's closest friends. He didn't do much associated with the school; instead, he enjoyed having fun and partying. He hadn't played organized sports for quite some time because he would rather spend his days with his girlfriend Brittany, and his nights drinking or just enjoying life. He lived on Lake Norman, and was fortunate enough to reside in the biggest house on the lake, where he gladly opened up his home for parties whenever his parents were out of town.

Ben was one of the richest kids at Parkside because his parents owned multiple businesses, which at one point, included a significant portion of the land that made up the lakefront. He was truly spoiled and didn't understand the value of hard work as everything had been handed to him throughout his entire life. Many of the Parkside students did whatever Ben asked of them, just because of his parent's wealth, which made for a dangerous situation. Ben had a good build, but wasn't nearly as in shape as the wrestlers he hung out with. None the less, he had a charm about him and a way with words that regularly kept him out of trouble. Besides, he was usually the person pulling the strings, causing others to get into trouble instead of himself.

Ben almost never went anywhere without his girlfriend Brittany Madison, who was the wrestling teams head score girl, which she had been doing since her freshman year. She traveled with the team and took score for Coach Tanzino as well as assisted in any way that she could. Brittany was an otherwise bright and nice girl, except for her poor judgment in dating Ben, who was only with her because of her beauty and the fact that she was sexually adventurous with him. Her long brown hair and dark complexion came from her Native American ancestry. Her dark eyes mesmerized those that looked into them and easily drew the attention of most of the boys at Parkside, but Ben's ability to shower her with lavish gifts and never ending supply of fun activities and events ultimately led her to him.

Brittany's best friend, Aisha Roberts, tagged along, because where you found one of them, you always found the other. She too helped as a score girl for the wrestling team, but she was mainly around to look at and flirt with the boys, an act that usually got her into trouble with Coach Tanzino. Coach was adamant that he didn't want his athletes distracted when they needed to focus on the task at hand. Aisha was African-American with a dark mocha complexion. Her hair was generally long as she usually had some type of extensions in. Her 5'7" athletic frame aided in her pursuits as a track athlete and soccer player, which led to her third place finishes, at the North Carolina State Championships, in both the 100 and the 200 yard dashes, just a month earlier.

As an assistant coach, Al Nelson's youthful exuberance and eagerness to do whatever it took to succeed went a long way in aiding the team towards reaching its goals. He valued the experiences of learning under Vincent's tutelage, which placed him in a position to gain knowledge from the best, while preparing the next generation of Parkside graduates. Al wrestled at Parkside High School and graduated after Anthony's freshman year. He was the senior captain of the wrestling team that posted an 8-8 record and the first team not to have a losing record in school history, which also coincided with Coach Tanzino's first season as the head coach. Although Al's teams hadn't experiences a lot of success throughout his career, Al was one of the lone bright spots as a four-year starter.

After graduating, Al received a scholarship to a local college that didn't have wrestling. This led Vincent to offer him the position as an assistant coach. This allowed him to remain a part of the sport and to help the team reach its ultimate goal of obtaining its first state championship. At times, he had trouble separating himself from the athletes that he coached, as he was only a couple of years older than them, but it was a skill that he was working on. He spent many hours observing everything that Vincent did as he tried to emulate the man that had given him such an amazing opportunity.

The Williams' residence, which was modest compared too many of the other homes that were located on Lake Norman, had a dock on the water, which held their boat and two jet skis. Their residence was a two story 2,700 square foot brick home with hardwood floors throughout. Upstairs was the kitchen, living room, master bedroom, an office with a spare bed, and a spare bedroom for guests. The basement was almost its own residence as it had its own small kitchen, workout room, Anthony's bedroom, his bathroom, and a game room. The game room had a pool table, a dart board, and a large television. This was where Anthony and many of his friends regularly came to hangout. The basement was like Anthony's sanctuary, where he spent a lot of his time getting an extra workout in or when he wasn't training, thinking about his future or even attempting to get his mind off of cutting weight.

The house was beautiful, but the Williams' worked extremely hard to provide for Anthony and to live there, which was somewhat beyond their means. Anthony's parents tried to provide everything they could for him; including: wrestling camps, a comfortable place to live, and a life that neither of them had while growing up. They never wanted Anthony to struggle or to go without anything as he fulfilled his dreams. Their entire world was Anthony and he loved and respected them for providing him with as many opportunities to succeed as possible.

The six foot tall and slender Terrance Williams always located himself behind the grill, where he prepared the burgers, steaks, ribs, and chicken for all of their guests. He kept his hair short and neat as he was very professional in the way he dressed and acted. While the 5'6", petite, and very pretty Olivia, with her long black hair, and her olive complexion, worked on all of the sides for the meal and kept the drinks flowing for the adults. Even though she was nearly 40, her beauty had lasted as she could still pass for being in her twenties.

The kids spent most of their time either playing games or out on the lake tubing and riding the jet skis, while the Williams', Vincent, and Vanessa sat by the pool, grilling, drinking, and talking. The adults enjoyed their conversation and relaxation while Anthony and the others were on the lake. Anthony drove the boat, allowing everyone else to take turns riding the water skis and using the tubes. Ben was a bit of a daredevil when it came to being on the lake as he used one of the jet skis to jump the waves that were made by all of the boats. Everyone was in their bathing suits, working on their tans, while enjoying the sun and fun that the lake provided. They were a very close knit group of friends as each would do anything for the others.

After they had been out on the water for a while, they returned to the Williams' dock to go swimming. However, Anthony and Amanda had another idea as they took the boat back out onto the water in order to disappear and have some rare quality alone time.

Once Anthony and Amanda were far enough away from everyone and any other boat, they dropped the anchor. Anthony pulled Amanda close as he told her how much he loved her. Amanda immediately gave him a big kiss and replied, "I love you too

Anthony. I'm so proud of you and everything that you've accomplished, but I miss you so much when you're gone. I wish that we could spend more time together, but I know how important wrestling is to your future."

Anthony reciprocated her kiss as he held on tight to her, showing just how much she meant to him. "Wrestling is very important to me, but so are you," replied Anthony. "I wish I could spend more time around here just having fun, but I need to do whatever it takes to earn a full ride to college, so that my parents don't have to keep spending all of their money on me and enjoy life for themselves."

Amanda smiled as she added, "You know that doesn't bother them. They love being able to make a better life for you."

"I know, but I want them to do more for themselves. By earning a scholarship, that would allow them to save money, have some alone time, and start taking vacations."

"Yeah, a vacation to wherever you're wrestling," quipped Amanda as she laughed. "You know they're still going to spend their money following you and watching you wrestle in college, no matter if you stay close to home or go somewhere far away."

"At least they'd have the option of doing more for themselves. I just want to pay them back one day for everything that they've done for me."

Amanda leaned in close as she hugged Anthony and confidently told him, "You will."

Anthony knew that Amanda was somewhat bothered by the fact that he'd likely be leaving Charlotte and wanted her to know, "And don't worry about me going off to college and leaving you behind. I love you and want you in my life, no matter where I end up at."

This definitely worried Amanda, as she was fearful of losing her boyfriend and her best friend to some other woman. "I just worry sometimes that you're going to go away and forget all about me or find that college girls are prettier than me."

"Come on Amanda, you're so beautiful, why would I want another woman," assured Anthony. "Besides, I've never cheated on you and just because I might not be around you when I'm in college doesn't mean I'll start."

Amanda leaned in, kissed Anthony again and replied, "You're so sweet. I'm glad that you wouldn't."

It wasn't long before the two of them took advantage of this time together as they maneuvered onto the floor of the boat. This alone time gave Anthony and Amanda an opportunity to be intimate with each other, especially since they didn't get many chances to do so. Amanda missed Anthony and she wanted to show him just how much, by doing whatever she could to satisfy her boyfriend.

They sat there docked, letting the warm sun beat down on their bare skins. They enjoyed their time together, letting all of their inhibitions go as they pleased one another until both of them had fulfilled the others' needs. Unfortunately for them, they knew that they didn't have much time. Once they realized they'd been gone for a while, they decided that everyone might be looking for them, so they hastily got dressed and made their way back to the party.

The boat showed up to the dock just in time for dinner. The rest of the group had already gotten out of the water, toweled off, and were making their way around the smorgasbord of food that had been prepared for them. Everyone filled their plates to the brim, even though they knew that they'd be forced to go back for seconds by Mrs. Williams. The kids mingled with the adults as they sat on the patio furniture eating and talking. For the wrestlers, it was good to be eating whatever they wanted, as they knew that they wouldn't have to make weight again for two weeks, and they felt that one day off from cutting weight wouldn't hurt them in the long run.

After everyone gorged themselves with food, the plan was for the entire group to go back out onto the lake and enjoy the remainder of the sunshine. Then, they planned on sitting back and watching as the sun set, which would be followed by fireworks soon afterwards. The fireworks display was always something spectacular as the colors would reflect off of the water, showing a complete mirror image of what was being seen in the sky, making an amazing sight for anyone fortunate enough to get to experience it.

Everyone was already at the boat by the time Vincent and Anthony arrived. As Vincent had pulled Anthony aside to give him a quick lecture on using protection, because he noticed that Anthony and Amanda hadn't returned to go swimming with everyone else. Vincent was well aware of what they'd been doing when they disappeared, especially since he had heard too many details while in practice, in the locker room, or on trips with his team. Vincent was realistic, as he knew that teenagers were going to have sex. He just wanted to make sure that Anthony didn't ruin his chances of wrestling in college or earning an education by getting Amanda pregnant.

Vincent and Anthony got there just as Vanessa was taking off her tank top and shorts, for the first time that afternoon, revealing her skimpy bright pink two piece bikini. She possessed a beautifully toned silky smooth body, long black hair, and long legs, with an amazing petite yet athletic figure, and a face that rivaled any model or actress. As Vanessa showed off her exquisite body, Tim, Ben, Chris, and Anthony all became transfixed as they gazed upon her, which didn't go unnoticed.

Brittany jumped at the chance to call them out, "Hey boys, you might want to lift up your jaws, and stop drooling. You guys should be ashamed of yourselves for looking at Coach's girlfriend like that."

Everyone turned and looked at the guys who were clearly embarrassed for being caught. Vanessa and Vincent both smiled and laughed at the fact that Brittany had humiliated the guys as they were inappropriately gawking at Vanessa.

This gave Vanessa a hint of satisfaction, knowing that she was still desirable by men of all ages. While Vanessa was smiling, she told the guys, "Thanks for the compliment boys. I'm glad I haven't lost my touch."

Vincent immediately chimed in, "Okay guys, you can stop looking at my girl. Otherwise, there will hell to pay at practice."

Everyone laughed, even though they knew that Coach was serious. They instantly stopped looking at Vanessa as they didn't want to test Coach, especially since his practices were already hard enough. As the sun beat down on them, they enjoyed the weather, the water, and took turns riding behind the boat on the water skis. The group stayed out on the boat for a while, eventually stopping close to the house to drop anchor. All of the couples sat close to each other as they watched one of the wonderful views that God created. The sunlight began to fade, leaving the sky filled with a beautiful hue of yellow, orange, and red. It was a magnificent sight to see. However, the colors in the sky soon faded away, leaving darkness, except for what light came from the moon and the stars.

Once they had enjoyed the sunset, they headed back to the Williams' residence in order to get prepared for the rest of the evening. As the boat returned to the dock; Ben, Chris, Tim, Brittany, Aisha, and Al decided to leave and go to the local park by the high school so that they could watch the towns' firework display. They had plans to catch up with a few more friends, before enjoying some alcoholic beverages at Ben's house.

The remainder of the group stayed in the Williams' backyard to watch the fireworks that were going to be set off over the lake. The fireworks lit up the sky with red, white, and blue sparks. The explosions reflected off of the calm lake water providing for a remarkable sight. It was a perfect way to end what had been a spectacular day. Fortunately for them, the night was just beginning.

Once the fireworks display had concluded, the remainder of the group made their way inside the house to play a variety of games. As usual, the holiday parties included games and drinking for those that stayed over. Terrance began mixing up Strawberry Daiquiris for everyone, even Anthony and Amanda, as they started a heated game of Taboo. Anthony knew that he couldn't drink more than a couple, as he didn't want to derail his training in any way, or hinder his ability to win two more national championships in the coming weeks.

As the competition intensified, Vincent and Vanessa took a commanding lead over the others. The drinks continued to flow, the games got more entertaining and the laughs became louder and more frequent as everyone immensely enjoyed one another's company.

Vincent and Vanessa had grown to become family to the Williams' especially since they didn't have anyone else that could be considered as such anymore. In-spite of their families' irreconcilable differences, Terrance and Olivia never regretted their love as it had produced their wonderful son.

Like they usually did after any party at the Williams' residence, Vincent and Vanessa stayed in one of the spare bedrooms so that they didn't drink and drive. As everyone was big proponents of the act, and felt that nobody should ever do so. Amanda was also allowed, by her parents, to stay over at the Williams' house, but they kept her in a separate room as they didn't consent to Anthony and Amanda spending the night together under their roof. However, this usually didn't stop them from engaging in sexual relations after everyone else had gone to sleep, and tonight was no different.

Chapter Five

Freestyle and Greco-Roman Nationals
Fargo, North Dakota

July 12-16, 2014

Coach Tanzino's second season in charge of the Mustang Wrestling Club brought with it new heights of success. Vincent was proud to be associated with the team as he loved seeing his athletes improve and achieve the goals that they'd set out to accomplish. In the first season, the team had four members make the North Carolina Freestyle and Greco-Roman team that competed in Fargo, while the second season produced eleven in total, and one athlete, Anthony Williams, who was able to qualify in both styles.

The tournament that was held in Fargo was another way in which the athletes could compete against the best of the best from around the country. Giving them a measuring tool to see where they stacked up nationally in Freestyle and Greco-Roman while receiving further exposure to college coaches, as the event provided them with an opportunity to recruit some of the nation's most talented wrestlers.

Since so many of his athletes qualified to wrestle in Fargo, Vincent decided to invite all of the other North Carolina representatives to train with them at the Parkside facilities from July 12th to the 16th. Vincent felt as though this was a great bonding experience for the athletes, as they'd be representing their home state with pride. Many of the athletes and their coaches took Vincent up on his offer, as the Parkside Wrestling Room was filled to capacity with athletes who were hungry to earn a National Championship or at least place in the top eight.

The five day intensive training camp was mostly run by Vincent, but he gained input from various other veteran coaches, who were knowledgeable and had been through this process on several occasions. Each of the main coaches took turns running sessions, as the athletes participated in two a day workouts, and were even given the opportunity to do work on their own, as Vincent basically lived at the facility throughout the five days.

Vincent wanted to see North Carolina gain some recognition, not just for himself and his teams, but for the state as a whole. Because by doing so he felt it would allow more athletes coming out of North Carolina to be recruited. Vincent also felt that the more elite caliber athletes that the state produced, the better his team looked when they beat them.

The five days went off without a hitch, as many of the other coaches and athletes were grateful for Vincent's hospitality. Most of the participants reveled at the opportunity to gain some insight into the sport of wrestling from such an accomplished man. Vincent felt honored by the praise he received from the others, but for him, it was more about his athletes having an opportunity to train against even better competition, as all of the Mustang Wrestling Club athletes were invited to participate, not just the Fargo Qualifiers. Besides, it gave everyone more workout partners who possessed varying styles, strengths, experiences, and techniques, which would inevitably be useful while wrestling athletes from all over the Unites States.

July 17-26, 2014

On Thursday July 17th, the North Carolina Freestyle and Greco-Roman Teams traveled to Fargo, North Dakota for the National Championships that would be held over the next week and a half. The team arrived early enough to get settled in for a day before competition began on Saturday, July 19th.

Each day brought something new to the table as the different styles and age groups would be competing at various points throughout the week. Not everyone would wrestle each day, as the tournament was spread out to give the athletes who qualified in both styles, a fair chance at being successful. This also aided the coaches, who could focus more time and efforts on a couple of athletes a day, instead of an entire team.

Vincent felt good about his athletes being able to obtain success, but also realized that many would experience defeat, as the competition was like nothing else that they'd ever been involved in. However, in Vincent's eyes, this was the best experience that any of them could have. It was exactly what each wrestler needed to make them strive for more in the upcoming season. Yet, no matter the outcome, Vincent felt honored to be there working with such tremendous young men. Vincent wanted to make sure that they took the entire situation in and enjoyed it, instead of just focusing on wins and losses.

The tournament in Fargo was often considered the pinnacle of an athletes' career in high school. In-spite of Vincent high hopes for his athletes, he was realistic, knowing that many of them would be eliminated prior to advancing to the top eight. But, one athlete in particular, Vincent felt would undoubtedly earn numerous wins and hopefully a chance for at least one, if not two more national championships.

After winning the Folkstyle Nationals, Anthony Williams was on everyone's radar as a man to beat. He had yet to taste defeat throughout the off-season, and he was going to do everything in his power to keep it that way. But, there were plenty of obstacles in his way as he'd face formidable opponents in each match, who were eager to take a crack at him and anyone else who tried taking away what they coveted.

Throughout the week, the arena would be filled with future collegiate All-Americans, National Champions, and even Olympians as this event was known for showcasing athletes who'd become the future of the sport, which appeared to be extremely bright for the Unites States.

Tuesday: July 22, 2014

On Tuesday July 22nd, Anthony Williams and the remaining Junior Greco-Roman competitors would have their opportunity to earn a National Championship. It had been a grueling couple of days of competition leading up to the culmination of the event for athletes that had made it to the top eight. They had been tasked with wrestling against the best and had come out in a position to leave their mark on the sport. Only the top wrestlers remained in the final day to determine their placement in the nation. They had finally made it to the promise land as the best Greco-Roman wrestlers in the nation.

As the days progressed, Vincent watched as many athletes' hopes and dreams were dashed by another competitor. His athletes fared well, but by the time that the championship rounds were upon them, only one remained, Anthony Williams. Anthony continued his dominance as he repeatedly destroyed everyone in his way. He was on a warpath, as he tried to obtain his destiny. He felt as though it was in the stars and that fate ultimately wanted him to win and would do whatever was necessary to achieve that dream.

As the dust settled on the day, the championship matches were all set, and Anthony was in one of them. The 160 pound final pitted Anthony Williams against Steven Crest from Illinois, who was already committed to wrestle in college for his hometown Fighting Illini. Steven had just graduated high school, after winning two state championships, along with finishing second twice. He had been a highly sought after wrestler, especially by many of the teams in the Big 12 and the Big 10, both of which were two of the powerhouse collegiate conferences for wrestling.

Since Greco-Roman doesn't allow an athlete to touch the competitors' legs or use their own leg to complete a move, it challenges the athlete to fight for inside control to obtain an opportunity to throw their opponent or complete various other moves and holds with their upper body. Athletes generally worked on gaining inside control by using various hand fighting techniques, which in Greco-Roman was imperative to be good at. The competitors needed to use their upper body strength and their hips to be successful at completing the moves in their repertoire.

Anthony felt good with his hand fighting ability, as he and Coach Tanzino had many battles in practice which had prepared him for a moment just like this. After only 30 seconds of hand fighting and jockeying for position, Anthony snapped Steven's head down, immediately grabbing a front headlock. Once he had the front headlock securely fastened, and had maneuvered his opponent to the ground, he immediately proceeded to hit a gator roll, placing his opponent directly on his back. Anthony settled into position, as he had complete control of his opponents head and arm, while he rested perpendicularly in a chest-to-chest position.

The official quickly got down onto the mat, looked at the space, or lack thereof, between Steven's back and the mat, and slapped his hand on the mat, indicating that Anthony had pinned Steven Crest, earning him his second National Championship of the year, and first ever in Greco-Roman. This was by-far the quickest match of the championships as the heralded Steven Crest didn't even last a minute.

Once again, Anthony had accomplished one of his goals, but this one was different. He didn't celebrate this win as he had his Folkstyle National Championship, because he expected himself to win. Besides, he knew that he still had work to complete as he had another event to wrestle in and another championship to achieve. After getting his hand raised, he gave a short hug to Coach Tanzino, grabbed his warm-ups, placing them back on, and ran to the warm-up area to get another workout in, since he felt as though the finals match hadn't challenged him enough. He was completely focused and determined to achieve, what most athletes couldn't even fathom, a Triple Crown.

Saturday: July 26, 2014

Anthony easily maintained his weight throughout the week long competition. Since he wasn't really cutting much weight, Anthony felt fresh and ready to go as the final day of the competition arrived for him. On Saturday, July 26th, a Junior Freestyle National Championship would be won by the lucky few. Anthony felt confident that he'd be joining that list. He had already won the first two legs of the Triple Crown, the Folkstyle and the Greco-Roman National Championships, and he was poised to win the last one.

The Mustang Wrestling Club had five of their eight Freestyle athletes competing in the Junior Division of the event, while the other three had already wrestled in the Cadet portion of the tournament. The three of them had done well, especially Matt States who won a few matches, but none of them had reached the championship rounds. However, the Junior Division was different as they were led by Anthony Williams, Tim Ridley, and Chris States. Each of which experienced a tremendous amount of success.

Throughout the first three rounds, each of them didn't appear to be competing against the opponents that were on the mat with them. Instead, they were competing with each other as they challenged one another to be even better. If one of them earned a decision, another one tried to outdo their friend by earning a tech-fall or even a pin. It was a healthy competition amongst them, which seemed to be working in their favor. None of it was done in malice as each wanted to watch their teammates and best friends succeed. They just wanted to bring more incentives to the table.

The fourth round brought a new set of challenges as Chris was the first to taste defeat. Afterwards, he earned one more victory in the wrestle backs, before being eliminated just two rounds shy of making it to the top eight in the 120 pound weight class. This was an accomplishment that was beyond what many would have expected. His valiant effort had given him an incredible experience and confidence that Coach Tanzino knew would transition into an extremely promising senior season.

Tim was able to win his fourth round match, before being defeated in the quarterfinals, and then eliminated in the round of twelve of the wrestle backs. To Tim, it was a major success, especially considering that he'd spent most of the off-season playing baseball instead of wrestling. He was pleased, and even though he wanted to play baseball in college, he was being recognized as someone that had the potential to wrestle collegiately if he decided otherwise, or possibly in certain circumstances, do both.

This left Anthony as the lone athlete remaining to place in the top eight of the tournament, but he wanted to do even better than that, he wanted to win. He continued to show his dominance as he made his way to the semifinals against Jose Martinez, who was a California native and already committed to wrestle at Arizona State. Martinez was making his third appearance in the semifinals at Fargo, but had yet to find his way into the championship match, as he always found himself running head on into the eventual champion, which Anthony was hoping to once again be the case.

Anthony and Jose battled back and forth throughout the match, and with only 30 seconds left, the score was tied at 4-4. Each athlete had made their best attempts to break the tie, but neither was able to do so until Anthony used one of Coach Tanzino's signature moves to bust the match wide open. Anthony worked to obtain inside control, by having both of his hands cupped onto Jose's shoulders. Once he was on the inside of Jose's arms, he faked a duck under to his right, only to come back and hit one on the left. Jose wasn't able to react quickly enough as Anthony found himself behind his opponent, with his arms wrapped around Jose's waist. Anthony immediately sunk his hips down, so that they were positioned below his opponents, before using the power in his legs to lift Jose up off of the mat and launch him backwards.

Jose flew through the air, landing squarely on his back, as Anthony had just hit a suplex, and with it, four points. But he didn't rest there. As Jose maneuvered to his stomach, Anthony kept a firm grip around his opponents' waist and immediately hit a gut wrench, causing Jose to roll from his stomach to his back before returning to his stomach again. With the two additional points, Anthony blew the score wide open as he now had a commanding 10-4 lead. Anthony played it safe as the last remaining seconds ticked off the clock. He had just advanced to the finals and was only one win away from achieving greatness. Only the elite of the elite were able to win all three National Championships, and Anthony was on the cusp of becoming one of them.

All Anthony had left to do was to beat Chase Hadley, the third ranked wrestler in the nation at 160 pounds. Chase was heading into his senior season of high school, in Pennsylvania, but had already committed to wrestle in college at Penn State; just like his older brother, his uncle, and his father had previously done. His families' participation in the sport led Chase to have over a decade of experiences as a wrestler and an unmatched wealth of knowledge at his fingertips. But Anthony didn't care about any of that, as he was determined to showcase his talents and to catapult his name to the top of the national rankings.

Meanwhile, back in Parkside, a number of friends, teammates, and fans gathered at Ben's house to watch Anthony compete for the Triple Crown. Ben had bought a membership to FloWrestling, an online organization that allowed wrestling fans a chance to stream major events live. After Anthony had won his second National Championship, only a few days earlier, Ben immediately called everyone together to watch the event in the movie room at his house. It was an enormous room, filled with oversized comfortable leather chairs and a ridiculously large screen. Ben had been watching all week long leading up to the party. He saw his friends' triumphs and tribulations as he also watched a number of Chris and Tim's matches. Everyone was ecstatic over Anthony's semifinal success, but hoped that he'd earn one more win.

The group had their food and drinks in hand as the footage streamed live in front of them. They watched on the giant screen, as Anthony stepped onto the mat, with a determination about him that none of them had ever seen before. His focus was clear to anyone who was watching, and they for one wanted to see him succeed. Everyone cheered him on as if they were there live and he could actually hear them. The group took pictures and Tweeted live throughout the match to everyone in the Parkside community that wasn't watching the match, as they were proud of their hometown hero.

As the referee blew his whistle to start the match, Anthony didn't waste a second before going on the offensive. He began relentlessly attacking, never giving Chase an opportunity to breath. After two attempts at a takedown had been thwarted, Anthony set up and hit a blast double, just like one of his idols, Jordan Burroughs, who was famous for it and a man who had represented the United States with pride and ferocity, enough so that he won an Olympic Gold Medal and two World Championships thus far in his illustrious career. The blast double looked exactly like one that Burroughs would hit, as Anthony had studied film on the legends most recognizable move, in order to perfect it himself.

The takedown gave him two points, but he wasn't satisfied, as he immediately hit a gut wrench on his opponent, gaining him two more points and an early 4-0 lead in the match. Once the referee placed them back onto their feet, Anthony continued to attack Chase, causing him to back away almost the entire time instead of setting up his own moves. Anthony was full of confidence, almost feeling unstoppable. He knew that he wouldn't be denied from earning this championship.

As the time was running out on the first period, Anthony continued to push the pace of the action, while Chase continued to back away. With ten seconds left, Anthony took two quick shots, both defended by Chase, but in doing so, he stepped backwards and out of bounce. As Chase stepped out, he was hit with a penalty point, giving Anthony one more point for the push out, and a 5-0 lead going into the break.

Thus far, the match couldn't have gone any better for Anthony, while Chase hadn't experienced anything like it. Nobody had ever been this aggressive or completely dominated him like this before. Chase was stunned by everything that had happened in the first period, especially considering there was a National Championship on the line.

As the second period began, both athletes were on their feet, but this time Chase was determined to move forward and take some risks, but his forward motion only aided Anthony. As soon as Chase placed his left hand on Anthony's shoulder, Anthony grabbed a Russian tie-up, and immediately stepped his left leg in-between Chase's legs in order to hit an inside trip. Chase fell to the mat, but as he did, he bellied out, causing his stomach to hit the mat instead of his back. Anthony was now up 7-0 and in complete control.

Chase did everything he could to prevent Anthony from hitting any other moves, but it wasn't enough. Anthony maneuvered to grab a reverse gut wrench, leaving his arms facing backwards and tightly locked underneath Chase's stomach. He used all of his strength and power in his hips to lift Chase up off of the mat, before launching him in the air. Chase went from seeing the mat, to seeing the ceiling lights, back to seeing the mat again, as Anthony hit a superb throw. The official deemed it as a grand amplitude move, as Chase had been lifted high enough off of the ground and landed with his back exposed to the mat and in danger of the fall, before the momentum caused him to make his way to his stomach. The official held up four fingers as he blew his whistle to stop the match. With those four points, Anthony had earned an 11-0 technical fall win over the highly regarded Chase Hadley.

Anthony stood in the center of the mat, as the official raised his arm. This allowed everyone in the arena to observe a rare Triple Crown winner, as they clapped and cheered loudly for him. Anthony had achieved what he had set out to do, win every major championship, while going undefeated throughout the off-season. He enjoyed this win even more than he had the previous two championships, as he realized that he had done something that only a select few had ever done. He was now the newest member of an elite group of wrestlers.

Anthony ran over to Coach Tanzino, and gave him a huge bear hug, lifting him off of the mat, as the adrenaline and the juices in his body still coursed through his veins. As he let Coach go, he immediately ran over to his parents who were nearby in the stands, giving both of them a big hug, allowing the Williams' to embrace their son. They were so proud of everything that he had accomplished. It was even beyond their wildest dreams, as he had just finished his third year as a wrestler, and he was already a three-time National Champion.

While Anthony was hugging his parents, the slightly delayed FloWrestling feed finally showed the last few seconds of the match. Everyone at Ben's erupted as they watched Anthony launch his opponent into the air, earning four points and the victory. They all toasted to his Triple Crown, with three shots of Crown Royal each, representing each leg of his accomplishment, and a way for them to honor their friend. They were all proud to be friends with Anthony, as they couldn't wait for him to get home and to celebrate all of his accomplishments. Ben immediately set in motion plans to have another party to honor their friend, which everyone agreed was a great idea.

They weren't alone in the excitement of the moment, as the wrestling community was in a buzz for the rest of the day, as they had just witnessed an athlete, who many now believed to be the next best thing to come out of the United States, do the unthinkable. They knew that whatever university landed this young man was going to have an absolute stud on their hands, and someone who would likely win multiple collegiate National Championship and possibly even World Championships for the United States.

After returning home from his historic Triple Crown run, Vincent and Anthony were bombarded with phone calls in regards to Anthony's future. He had made quite a name for himself, enough so that he was being offered scholarships. He had received offers for a full-ride to the University of Buffalo, Campbell University, and North Dakota State; while he was offered partial scholarships from West Virginia University, UNC-Chapel Hill, NC State, Appalachian State, Missouri, and Iowa State.

Anthony was also given an opportunity to walk-on to several programs with the option of earning a scholarship as his performance proved he deserved it. The invited walk-on offers came from Oklahoma State, Iowa, Penn State, Arizona State, Davidson, and Maryland. All of which gave Anthony a lot to think about. Enough so that he had a number of conversations with his parents and Coach Tanzino about his options.

Anthony felt blessed to be receiving such offers from so many wonderful schools, but he wanted to make sure that he made the right decision. But the right decision had to have a full-ride attached to it, and be the school of his choice, in order to alleviate the financial burden from his parents. He was hoping, that with an amazing senior season, that he'd be able to turn the partial scholarships and some of the invited walk-on opportunities into full scholarships. He liked the universities that had offered him a full scholarship, but he just wanted to make sure whatever school he decided on, gave him every opportunity to win as a wrestler and to earn a degree of his choice.

Anthony was well aware that it was a gamble to wait and not make a decision right away, especially since he had three colleges offering a full scholarship already. Yet, in-spite of the possibility of getting injured or worse, Anthony was willing to bet on himself as he planned on showing everyone that he was the best wrestler coming out of the class of 2015.

After Anthony's decision to remain unsigned for the time being, Vincent called his friend, Don Simpson, who was an Assistant Coach at West Virginia University. They spent a lot of time talking about Anthony and the potential for him to earn a full-ride to the school. Don was willing to do so, only if Anthony was able to go undefeated throughout his senior year and win a state championship. But, to Don, Anthony was going to have to continue to do so in an impressive fashion, as he and the rest of the coaching staff needed to be wowed a little more before giving a full-ride to an incoming athlete, especially considering that they only had 9.9 scholarships available to the whole team, not just the incoming freshman. The restrictions on the number of scholarships that college wrestling programs have make it challenging to find an appropriate balance between incoming talent and veteran presence on the team. Which was why so many colleges were willing to offer invited walk-on experiences or partial scholarships, to make sure they get the most out of their limited scholarships.

Vincent was pleased with his conversation, as he knew that this could be great for Anthony. But Vincent didn't have any plans on letting Anthony know about this right away, as he wasn't going to add any additional pressure to the young man who had good intentions into why he wasn't going to sign any offer at this time. Vincent liked Anthony's maturity with this decision, as his devotion to his parents was commendable. Anthony was only looking to ease his parents' financial burden; ultimately repaying them for all that they had done for him over the years.

Chapter Six

The School Year Begins

Monday: August 25, 2014

In North Carolina, August 25th signifies the end of the summer and the beginning of a new school year. Students and teachers usually hated the return of school as it meant that work had to be completed once again, while parents looked forward to it. But one person in particular was happy to be back. Anthony was excited for the first day of his senior year as it meant that he was one day closer to the beginning of wrestling season; a season that promised to produce numerous accolades and endless possibilities for a bright future.

The beginning of the school year also signified that the new national and state rankings were published. To the surprise of nobody, Anthony Williams was atop them in many categories. He was slated as one of the top 10 wrestlers in the nation for all levels of high school. Anthony was also the number one recruit in the 160 pound weight class nationally and the number five overall for all upcoming seniors. His national ranking was significantly higher than Jamie Wright; however, Anthony was still ranked second to him in North Carolina. Many in the state believed that Jamie was the wrestler to beat until Anthony could actually beat him, while national voters anticipated that Anthony was a much bigger prospect and would have the better collegiate career.

As the 1,500 students filed into Parkside High School, none were as popular as Anthony. He had the benefit of being the king of the school. As the king, he had free reign of whatever he wanted and could do no wrong with the faculty and staff. Anthony took advantage of the freedom that he was afforded by being the star athlete and someone with a 3.8 GPA. But, he never let it get to his head or caused any problems for anyone, as he was taught to be respectful of others, especially his elders. Instead, he was a peacemaker and convinced others to forgive and forget; which was an odd demeanor to have as a championship caliber athlete who trained on a daily basis to physically dominate and demolish his opponents.

As his senior year began, Anthony only needed a few credits to graduate, which gave him a chance to take Advanced Placement courses in order to earn college credits. He knew the importance of having a head start as it provided him with an opportunity to earn college credits at a much cheaper rate and, due to his grades, afforded him the freedom to be accepted into any university of his choice.

As he walked around the halls of Parkside, Anthony had an air of invincibility and confidence that was never misconstrued as arrogance. All of the girls wanted to date him and all of the guys wanted to be him. The attention that Anthony received from all of the females at the school sometimes bothered Amanda, but she was sure that her boyfriend wouldn't do anything to betray the trust and love that they'd forged over the past year. The endless supply of women tempting him never led Anthony to stray, because he knew what a gem he had in his loving girlfriend. His influence was obvious to all who saw him walk through those halls; however, he never took it too far, because if he did, he knew that his parents and especially Coach Tanzino would be on his case.

As the students sat in their first period classes conversing before the school year officially began, Dr. Gordon's voice came over the loud speaker, "Attention students, this is your principal speaking. We'd like to welcome you all back to Parkside High School, after what I'm sure was a very enjoyable summer vacation. But now it's time to open those books and dedicate the proper amount of time to your studies. We have high expectations that all of you will follow your teachers' instructions and put forth the effort necessary to earn grades required to attend an institution of higher learning.

"I know that we will have a great academic school year as well as many successes with our athletic programs. We hope to see all of you participate with one or more of our sport teams. If not, we hope that you'll be in the stands cheering on our wonderful student athletes and your friends.

"On that note, I'd like to congratulate Anthony Williams on all of the successes he had throughout the summer as he achieved three National Wrestling Championships and is now ranked as the best wrestler in the nation at 160 pounds. When you see him in the hallway, congratulate him and let him know that you're supporting him. Good luck to each and every one of you. I hope that I won't be seeing you in my office unless it's for me to praise you on a job well done."

As the day went on, Anthony felt as though every Parkside student congratulated him and wished him good luck on the upcoming season. It almost felt as though the weight of the school was on his shoulders and he had to talk to someone about it. He usually did his best work when the pressure was on him, but something seemed different today. So, he turned to the only person that knew how this felt and could help him out, Coach Tanzino.

Instead of going to lunch, Anthony headed to Coach Tanzino's classroom, which was located near the back of the school, near the practice facility. His room had athletic posters with inspirational quotes on them plastered all over the walls. Amidst the athletic posters, Coach Tanzino had the students' assignments and responsibilities written on his board, as he expected just as much out of them as he did his athletes. As Anthony entered the room, he was greeted with a firm handshake and a warm hug.

It wasn't unusual for Anthony to stop by his room, but today was different. Vincent knew exactly why Anthony was paying him a visit, "You're here to talk to me about the announcement aren't you?"

"Yeah, how did you know?" wondered Anthony.

"I know you, you want to beat everyone that steps on the mat with you, but you could care less if anyone else is there to watch besides your parents, Amanda, or myself. All of this hoopla is unnecessary in your eyes. You just want to focus on the task at hand and be congratulated once you've accomplished your goals, not before."

Anthony knew that Coach was right, but there was more to it, "True, but it's more than that Coach. I feel as though I'll disappoint everyone if I'm unsuccessful, almost like I have the weight of the entire school on my shoulders."

Vincent attempted to relieve some of the stress he was feeling, "But you don't. They're just here to support you, not put added pressure on you. Besides, the only person that you have to be worried about is yourself. If in the end, you can look yourself in the mirror and be confident that you gave your all, than you've done everything in your power. You're the only person that you have to make happy. You're the only person that you have to do any of this for."

Anthony swiftly replied, "Besides you and my parents. I want this for more than just myself Coach. I want to succeed to prove that you haven't wasted your time on me and that my parents haven't wasted so much money for me to be a failure."

Vincent understood the pressure that Anthony had placed on himself, "You won't be a failure, because you won't let yourself be one. And you've already made me extremely proud of you. I never think that I've wasted any time traveling or working out with you. If anything, I should thank you."

"For what," Anthony wondered.

Vincent winked as a big smile was plastered all over his face, "For keeping this old man in shape. I mean, I have to keep on my toes and remain in shape so that I can keep beating you in practice!"

Anthony laughed, "You got jokes now huh T.!"

"It's not a joke when it's true!"

Anthony confidently replied, "We'll see about that!"

And with that, Anthony walked out of Coach Tanzino's classroom with a smile on his face and feeling much better, as if some of the pressure had just been taken away from him. He knew that Coach was the right man to talk to as he always was. He had already been through much of what Anthony was experiencing as an athlete himself, so he knew how to deal with it. Besides, Anthony enjoyed having an opportunity to talk to Vincent. He wasn't just his coach or good friends with his family, he was family and even more so, he was his best friend. They had a bond that meant more to Anthony than he could explain. This man had given him so much and made tremendous sacrifices for him that Anthony wanted to do everything in his power to one day repay him.

Chapter Seven

Wrestling Team Meeting

Thursday: September 4th, 2014

At the beginning of September, Coach Tanzino always held an informational meeting for anyone interested in being on the wrestling team. Vincent felt that it was necessary to get started as early as possible to give his wrestlers a leg up against the competition. This included recruiting new athletes to join his program and getting his veterans back into shape prior to the start of the regular season.

Vincent had a grueling pre-season planned for anyone who wasn't currently playing another sport. He knew that this was the only way to improve on his athlete's strength and conditioning while teaching technique to the new wrestlers. The pre-season gave his veterans an opportunity to get back on the mat a couple of days a week and kick off the rust before the regular season began. Especially since Vincent had set up the teams schedule of matches and tournaments to be extremely arduous from the onset. He wanted to challenge his team from day one of the season and continue to do so throughout the year.

Vincent knew in order to produce champions that he'd have to challenge each athlete to be prepared for anything; which is why Coach Tanzino understood that if any of the wrestlers wanted to become the best, they'd have to repeatedly beat the best. Instead of just waiting until the end of the season to see elite competition, Vincent felt it would be beneficial to see those competitors early and often to prime his team for what was to come. Ultimately, allowing his athletes to be comfortable with wrestling against high level competition by the time it mattered the most; at regionals and states.

Coach Tanzino's room was packed with athletes who wanted to be a part of the team. But, before Coach Tanzino got up to speak to those in attendance, Anthony wanted to saw a few words, "For those of you that don't know me, I'm Anthony Williams and I'm one of your team captains. I'm a three year starter and a three time state place-winner. Some of why I'm here today is because of my talent and determination, the rest is because of the man standing next to me, Coach Tanzino, or to us Coach T. Throughout the year, practices will be extremely difficult, but I know that each of you can make it through; because in the long run, it'll be well worth it when Coach leads us to a conference championship. It won't be easy as it takes a lot of dedication and desire to succeed, but in the end, as long as you stick it out, you'll be proud of what you've accomplished."

From the back of the room, Chris exclaimed, "Conference Champs, I like the sound of that!" Some laughter was heard from those that knew Chris well. While a smile formed on many of the veterans faces as they knew that it was well within their grasp.

Tim, who was sitting off to the side of the room, added, "Anthony's right, the practices are intense, but what doesn't kill you, only makes you stronger. We have all the pieces in place to make a serious run at every major championship this year and I for one want to be the best team around."

All of the wrestlers were excited at the opportunity that was in front of them. There was a buzz in the room as Vincent began to speak, "Thanks guys. They're right, practice is tough, but it's my job to prepare you to win. My training regimen is based on the ones I went through in college, giving you the benefit of my experiences. Before any of you decide that practice is too tough and you think about quitting, just know that practice only gets easier as the season progresses. Everyone has a chance to start on this squad, just show me you deserve to and beat those in your weight class and it's yours. I don't play favorites as I believe that everyone who puts in the effort deserves a chance at cracking the starting lineup. But, before we start our first of many pre-season practices, let me go over my twenty ways to train like a champion."

Coach Tanzino grabbed a stack of papers and passed out a copy to everyone. Each wrestler received a sheet of paper that was filled with actions that were necessary to succeed. They each perused the twenty points to training hard and winning as they received the paper.

It was almost like Coach Tanzino's wrestling commandments, or a how to manual for victory. This piece of paper was nothing new to the returners, as they had received it each year that they'd been on the team. Most of them had taking these points to heart, making sure that they followed them each and every day, as they knew that they'd produce the desired result; winning.

Parkside Wrestling
How to Train Like a Champ
By: Coach Vincent Tanzino

1) No short cuts! (Don't cheat yourself.)
2) Make your opponent quit first. (Never stop working!)
3) Keep fighting no matter if you're winning or losing. (Anyone can win on any given day.)
4) Workout early, often, and stay late. (Put in the time necessary to be victorious.)
5) Defeat one opponent, and then defeat another. (Just because you can beat one person, doesn't mean that you can beat everyone. Continue to challenge yourself.)
6) Control the head…control the beast. (Where the head goes, the body goes.)
7) Don't cheat your way out of a hold. (No wall, out of bounds, or other group should stop your wrestling.)
8) Always push the pace and keep the action going. (Never ease up or settle for a lead, because the lead can disappear just as easily as it appeared.)
9) Always train with wrestling in mind. (All of your lifting and running is done to benefit you on the mat.)
10) Always show strength, not weakness. (Look like you're never tired.)
11) Give your all, all of the time. (Heart, mind, and soul.)
12) Don't hold back while training. (Take risks. Without them, you won't get better.)
13) Take advantage of your opponents breaks. (You wrestle when they aren't.)

14) Start and finish a move with the same intensity. (Never ease up.)
15) Use the edge of the mat to your advantage, action doesn't stop until the whistle blows. (Score points when your opponent eases up or isn't fully wrestling.)
16) Make your opponent tired, no matter the situation. (Whether you're winning or losing.)
17) Less rest, more wrestling. (It's all about intensity!)
18) Never allow a partner to take away from your training. (You get out, what you put in. If your partner isn't working hard, make them work hard, or find a new partner.)
19) Less conversation, more wrestling. (Talk before or after practice, not during.)
20) Know that you're a winner! (Believe in yourself!)

Coach Tanzino went into great detail on how each of the twenty points played a major role in affording every wrestler with a chance to become a champion. Vincent did more than just coach wrestling; he understood the intricacies and the utmost importance of mental preparation. He knew that if your mind wasn't ready to be successful, than you wouldn't be. His philosophies were grounded on the ideals that being a top notch athlete took more than just practice, but a high level of confidence, yet, not arrogance. Those who believed that they were great, but didn't put in the hard work necessary to do so, might be good, but would never truly be great. Vincent knew that a well-balanced athlete was the best athlete. Athletes with talent, mental control, and the knowledge that they can win are more likely to succeed than someone who didn't possess those qualities. But Coach warned his athletes that being too over confident can be bad, because that could lead to an unexpected loss, which usually occurred at the most inopportune time.

Every athlete remained focused as they followed along while Vincent detailed his points. Mostly everyone in attendance seemed to understand what Coach Tanzino was explaining, especially the returners. Many even spent time reading this list over and over again throughout the season as they wanted to constantly remind themselves of what was needed to become a champion. A number of the veterans even taped them up in their lockers, so they could read them every day before practice, as a reminder of what was needed to achieve their goals.

After going into elaborate details on how each of the rules pertained to his program and the goals that each athlete would set for themselves in order to achieve their desired outcome, Coach ended his speech with one questions, "Can all of you do that?"

Everyone responded with a resounding, "Yes!"

Vincent smiled, as he was happy with the response, and then added, "Well, if nobody has anything else to say, let's go to practice."

Not a word was spoken, as nobody questioned any of Coach Tanzino's philosophies, especially since they had either seen or heard about the success that he had produced. Everyone who wasn't currently playing a fall sport grabbed their belongings and made their way to the wrestling room to get dressed for the first pre-season practice of the year. A buzz of excitement filled the air, as each athlete knew that they had a clean slate filled with endless possibilities in front of them.

Once the team had changed and everyone was ready, practice began. Coach Tanzino wanted to make sure to improve his team's strength and conditioning throughout the pre-season so that when the regular season began, everyone would be prepared for the intensity and high demands that would be placed on their bodies. He knew that he'd have to intertwine exercises that would improve all aspects of his athletes' body composition. By increasing their lean muscle mass, enhancing their conditioning, and combining it with his techniques, Coach Tanzino knew that he'd be able to produce elite athletes.

Vincent instructed the athletes to begin jogging around the two mats. He wanted to make sure to get a good sweat out of them. Coach Tanzino called out a number of exercises for them to complete, which they did on command. The new guys followed suit and paid attention to the veterans if they were unsure of what to do. As the wrestlers ran around the room, they completing a number of tasks; most of which were intended to increase the athlete's heart rate while stretching out their muscles, because he didn't want anyone to get hurt.

After a few exercises, Coach Tanzino paired up the wrestlers with someone close to their weight for the next set of tasks; which included: buddy carries, wheel barrels, and vertical push-ups. They followed those with regular push-ups, sit-ups, and superman's' on coach's cadence. By the time Anthony led the team in stretching, everyone was already covered in sweat as they enjoyed the quick break from the intense workout that had only begun.

After stretching, Vincent gave the team two minutes to get water before the next stage of practice would begin. The guys were already tired as they made their way to the water fountain to rehydrate before sweating it all out again. Afterwards, Coach Tanzino split the team into two groups, rookies and veterans. The rookies went with Al, as he was in charge of teaching the basics which included stance, setting up a single leg takedown and various ways in which to finish the takedown. Coach Tanzino took the veterans and went quickly through the old moves from the past couple of years. Coach Tanzino called out a move and, without a second thought, his veterans complied.

Today's focus was the Russian tie series. Every takedown was to be completed after grabbing a Russian tie and using it to set up the shot. They did doubles, inside trips, high crotches, and sweep single leg takedowns. In-spite of the wrestlers having been inactive for the past month and a half, the team looked crisp, as if they hadn't even missed a day of training; which may have been the case as many of them had continued to work out together since the end of the off-season program in July. Realizing how good his team already looked, a smile formed on Vincent's face, as he discerned that this year would be a record breaking one for his team.

To end practice, they went through a number of conditioning activities. Coach Tanzino had the team run sprints on the track, followed by stadium steps. Each exercise was followed by push-ups, sit-ups, or some other activity intended to build his teams' strength. They also used their teammates' weight as they carried them up the steps of the stadium. This was meant to burn their leg muscles and increase their cardiovascular levels. All of which would better prepare them to succeed in an intense match.

As the conditioning came to an end, most of the team was irrefutably exhausted as they could barely sit up to stretch again. However, Anthony was ready to keep working out. After stretching with the team, he immediately went into the weight room to get a lift in, as he felt like he had more in the tank. He knew that the more time and effort he put in before the season started, that it would build up his conditioning and his skills to produce his desired results.

He wasn't alone, as Tim, Chris, Al, and Vincent all joined Anthony in the weight room. All of them had a burning desire to win a state championship and knew what it would take to do so. This was only the beginning of what appeared to be the hardest pre-season that Vincent had put his team through, but one that would undeniably pay huge dividends in the long run for the Parkside Mustangs.

Chapter Eight

Wrestling Season Begins

Wednesday: October 29, 2014

The first official day of the season was upon Parkside High School, which meant that the nearly three week grind of the beginning of the season had finally arrived. After a tough, but extremely productive pre-season, the wrestlers were excited about the regular season getting underway. Roughly half of the team had been present during the pre-season, while the other half participated in football, soccer, or cross-country, which meant that the entire team was in decent shape. However, everyone knew that the only way for someone to truly be in shape for wrestling was to actually wrestle.

In the North Carolina pre-season rankings, Parkside had three wrestlers in the top five. Chris States was ranked fifth at 120 pounds. Tim Ridley was ranked third at 170 pounds, while Anthony Williams was ranked second in the state at 160. As a team, Parkside was ranked second in the Mid-West Conference and twelfth overall in the state. This was the highest pre-season ranking for the wrestling team in school history.

Much of it was due to only graduating one senior from the previous season's team that saw them place second in the Mid-West Conference. It was also due in part to the success of the team at the 2014 State Championships, which had four out of five of the Parkside wrestlers place in the top six, which was also where they finished as a team.

Even though his team and athletes were highly ranked, Vincent was upset as to where they were, as he knew that his team was leaps and bounds better than what was being predicted. But that didn't matter, as wins and losses came on the mat, not from some writers' arbitrary opinion. Besides, this just gave Vincent more fuel for the fire as he could use it to motivate his athletes and himself.

As soon as the bell rang to announce the end of the day, the wrestlers quickly made their way to Coach Tanzino's room for a mandatory study hall. If the wrestlers didn't show up within five minutes of the bell, they knew that there'd be serious consequences in practice, and nobody wanted that. As the wrestlers arrived, they immediately began working on their homework because they were fully aware of the importance that Coach placed on their education.

While they were working, Coach Tanzino passed around a sign-up sheet for their first individual meeting of the year. This was a meeting for the wrestlers to get to know coach, and for coach to get to know them better. This was also a time for Vincent to assist each wrestler with setting their short and long term athletic and academic goals. Coach Tanzino wasn't just concerned with how they did on a wrestling mat, but he also cared about their academic progress. He wanted to ensure that they remained eligible and earn grades that would allow them to go to college.

Coach Tanzino held these meetings two to three times a year, but his door was always open if any of his athletes needed his help on anything or to readjust the goals that they'd previously set. Vincent cared about his athletes on and off the mat, as he knew most would never compete at the collegiate level. However, he wanted every one of his wrestlers to go to college because he knew the importance of an education and how it could further their lives.

Coach Tanzino had a strong desire to have his athletes succeed in all aspects of their lives, which is why he took an interest in everything that was going on. Vincent realized that some parents or guardians didn't set as high of a value on education as they should. So, he felt as though it was his responsibility to be a positive male role model and influence for each student-athlete that he had the opportunity to work with. Vincent made sure to encourage his athletes and teach them about life, not just wrestling. He did the same in the classroom as he always challenged his students to strive for more and to work hard at achieving what they wanted out of life, even pushing them to think outside the box or to have bigger dreams for themselves.

Each wrestler took their turn speaking to Coach Tanzino and writing down their short and long term goals. Some goals were to make the starting line-up while others wanted to win a state championship. Coach never discouraged his athletes, no matter how small or large the goals were. However, at times, he encouraged or challenged them to dig deeper and strive for more. A number of the goals weren't even related to wrestling as some of his athletes wanted to improve on their grades so that they'd remain on the team or to make the grades needed to get into college. Coach did everything he could to assist his athlete's academic goals by having study hall and finding tutors or other forms of assistance if his student-athletes needed it.

Once Coach had spoken to each wrestler, it was time for the first practice of the regular season to begin. Vincent stood in front of the room and called out instructions, "Dante, you get to mop the mats, Matt and Gary you're on water duty. Remember, everyone will have their opportunity to mop and get the water, except for my seniors, but if it doesn't get done, then I'll allow my captains to run practice for part of a day to help convince the rest of you the importance of your duties and responsibilities."

After Coach Tanzino's final instructions, the team gathered their belongings and made their way to the locker room to get changed. Dante grabbed the mop and the bucket and filled it with soap, water, and a little bit of bleach to properly clean the mat. He had done this many times as a freshman, so he was familiar with the process. Dante was the schools' star running back and Anthony's backup. And, as only a sophomore, he had a bright future ahead of him. His speed, agility, and aggressiveness on the football field gained him tremendous recognition by a number of colleges who already coveted his services. All of these skills, along with his athleticism, translated well onto the mat.

Dante Adams was 5'9" and generally weighed around 175 pounds during football season, but cut to 160 during the winter. He knew that he wouldn't see much action as a starter, but he'd see some opportunities in the starting lineup as he had done so during his freshman year. Vincent felt as though Dante was talented and athletic enough that he could win quite a few matches for the team, if he had to slot him in at 160 or 170, depending on what was needed by the team on any given night.

Coach Tanzino was known to bump his athletes around to different weight classes in order to win a match, which even included Anthony. Besides, some other coaches would try to prevent their athletes from wrestling Anthony, by either forfeiting or moving their wrestler to a higher weight class to avoid the matchup.

This made for a chess match between coaches and one that Vincent had become very skilled at winning. Vincent's plan for the season was if their opponents would try to forfeit or put their backup in at 160, and the opposition had to put their wrestler out their first, then Dante would receive the forfeit or wrestle the lesser opponent and Anthony would wrestle at 170, causing Tim to move to 182. This was a strategy that Vincent knew would worked extremely well for the Mustangs, as Dante would likely win most of his opportunities, but not in the way that Anthony did, at least not yet.

Once the mat was clean and the team was dressed, the first official practice of the season began. Coach Tanzino had the wrestlers start by running in a large circle around the room. The room was state of the art as it possessed two full wrestling mats, providing the team with ample space to complete all of Coach Tanzino's requests.

There were pads on the walls to prevent injuries from occurring, a closet which contained the mop and bucket, the medicine kit, extra mat tape, headgear, singlet's, knee pads, wrestling shoes, and various other supplies. The water fountain was next to the closet, along with a table that housed a cooler and several water bottles, for those occasional water breaks. Spread across the wall were pictures of state qualifiers, 100 match winners, team pictures, painted portraits of wrestlers in various holds and many other records. All of which had increased significantly over the past few years under Coach Tanzino's tutelage. His desire to build a powerhouse was well on its way and the possibilities seemed endless.

There was also a chart on the wall that showed who the starter and back-ups were in each weight class. The state of the art facility also housed weights, various cardiovascular machines, pull-up bars, a stereo, and a Television with a DVD player. All of which, were vastly better than any other school in the area and tremendously aided the team in achieving the success that they had enjoyed over the past few seasons.

Coach Tanzino led the team in calisthenics as he wanted to properly warm them up before the intense practice that was to follow. Vincent enjoyed the beginning of the season, as it was a time to see what each athlete was made of, before the grind of having to make weight was upon them. Unfortunately, this was also a time to weed out the athletes who didn't have what was needed to last as a wrestler. Coach held no animosity towards anyone who felt as though wrestling wasn't for them, as he knew how difficult of a sport it was. He tried encouraging anyone who wanted to quit to give it another chance, but if they truly felt as though it wasn't a good fit, Coach would let them go on their way as he didn't want someone who didn't want to be there to drag the rest of the team down. Ultimately, Coach knew that practice was just a precursor to the exhilarating portion of the season; competition.

Once the team was properly warmed up, Anthony led the team in stretching. Everybody was already covered in sweat as they enjoyed the few minutes of rest, before the inevitable challenges of practice occurred. Everyone was mentally prepared for the difficult practice to follow, or at least they thought they were. The few wrestlers that were new and hadn't gone through the pre-season practices were in for quite a surprise as they'd find out first hand just how difficult the next hour and a half would be on them.

As the seconds ticked away from their three minute water break, everyone quickly ran onto the mat, because if they weren't all back on the mat as time ran out, then they'd immediately begin conditioning for wasting Coach Tanzino's time. Coach did this as he wanted everyone to realize the value and importance of time. Vincent knew that every second of a match counted, especially when competing against the best of the best, so he wanted to ingrain the value of taking advantage of every moment into his athletes.

After the water break, Coach Tanzino split the team into two groups, the rookies and the veterans so that they could work at the proper pace needed. Just as they did in the pre-season, Al took the rookies, while Vincent took the veterans. Once each rookie showed that they had earned an opportunity to join the veterans, they'd be incorporated into their side of the practice mat. Coach hoped that within the first week or two that everyone would be practicing the entire time together. Vincent used this as a way to motivate the rookies to strive towards joining the veterans. He also felt as though it separated talent levels, which made for a smoother practice as it wasn't too boring for the veterans and wasn't too fast for the rookies.

As Vincent took control of the veterans, he always challenged them to improve on areas that could be considered weaknesses that an opponent might try to capitalize on. In many cases it was learning or even just improving on moves they'd use in a match, while others tried to perfect the moves that they already knew, but from the opposite side. Coach Tanzino recognized that this made his wrestlers more versatile and considerably more difficult to beat. He understood that each opponent was different and that various styles provided numerous challenges; however, if his wrestlers prepared for all contingences, then they'd be ready for any unexpected situations that arose within each and every match.

After drilling moves, Coach Tanzino had the team set up what he referred to as "Stations." It was a plyometric workout that increased the teams conditioning while allowing his athletes to improve or at least maintain their strength throughout the season. Fifteen stations were set-up around the room and the clock was set to 35 minutes. This allowed for the team to run through the stations twice along with some running in-between. Each athlete would rotate through, taking 45 seconds to continuously complete the exercise in front of them prior to taking a 15 second rest while moving to the next station and then beginning the process all over again. The stations included box jumps, dips, bicep curls, ball throws, squats, partner shots with exercise bands and a number of other activities that varied depending on the day or the time of the year.

By the time the 35 minutes had elapsed, each athlete was completely exhausted from a difficult day of practice. Yet, they knew that their training wouldn't be over until they completed additional conditioning and then finished up with stretching. Today's conditioning consisted of timed sprints on the mats. Each member of the team had to complete every sprint in a certain amount of time; otherwise, the sprint wouldn't count and everyone would have to do it over again. Fortunately for them, everyone made the required time on each sprint, preventing additional work to be added to the already draining practice. Vincent felt good about what he'd seen on the first day, as he believed it to be a positive sign of things to come and a season that would undoubtedly be filled with success beyond even his wildest dreams.

Chapter Nine

Animal Ball

Friday: November 14, 2014

After two weeks of grueling practices, Coach Tanzino felt that the team had finally earned the right to play one of their favorite games, Animal Ball. Animal Ball was a mixture of wrestling, basketball, handball, football, and soccer. The goal was to; through the help of your teammates, place the nerf ball onto the opposing teams' target on the opposite corner of the mat. They had to take continuous shots across the mat as the only way for them to move from one area to another. The participants were allowed to tackle each other, wrestle each other and tie one another up. They were also able to pass the ball from one teammate to another, but if the ball went out of bounds, then the other team had the opportunity to throw the ball in. The winner was always the first team to reach 15 points. The games were extremely intense, but fun. Everyone enjoyed playing Animal Ball and did everything they could to win as the winners were given the privilege of controlling five minutes of additional conditioning for the losing squad.

One of the rules that needed to be followed was that each wrestler couldn't get up off of their knees, nor could they crawl on the mat. They had to take continuous shots across the mat and if they didn't, their team would be penalized by losing possession of the ball. Rising up out of the continuous shots, or crawling, was similar to a traveling violation in basketball and caused one team to turn the ball over to the other.

To start the game, the ball was placed in the center of the mat and the whistle was blown for both teams to charge at the ball, through the use of continuous shots, in order to gain possession. Prior to attacking, each team started the possession kneeling behind a designated line that was close to their goal and opposite the other team. Teams would setup offensive and defensive players and formations in order to score or protect their goal. As the games got heated, so did the room. By the time the game ended, everyone would be drenched in sweat. Coach Tanzino felt as though the skills and the conditioning prepared his wrestlers to acquire the ability to work through uncomfortable or even awkward positions that they'd be placed in during their matches.

Whenever Coach Tanzino played, it was a distinct disadvantage to the opposing team as he was quicker than anyone on the mat and had moves as if he was back in his days as a running back in high school. Coach was able to control, and sometimes even tie up as many as three of the opposing players, thus, freeing up his own team and allowing for mismatches. He was even known to maneuver or power his way through the entire opposing team to score a goal all by himself, if he chose to do so.

The only player that even had a chance to compete with Coach Tanzino was Anthony, but most of the time they played on the same team, which ended up allowing them to dominate the competition. When Anthony was on the opposite team, Coach Tanzino had to play a one-on-one game against him, which left everyone else to battle one another. It became a situation, like most practices, where the two of them fought hard, yet Coach always found a way to win. In the end, his knowledge, experience, and years of wrestling were usually too much for Anthony to handle. However, Coach Tanzino didn't always play as he wanted to provide everyone with a chance at winning, since he had a distinct advantage and never lost a game.

Since Vincent didn't play in the first game of the season, Anthony's team, laden with veterans, took a commanding lead and eventually came away victorious. Anthony led the five minute conditioning session giving the losing team up-downs, sprawls, Coach's shuffle drill and a number of push-ups and sit-ups to do. Vincent didn't see this extra work as a punishment for losing, but more of a motivational tool to push his athletes to work harder and ultimately come away victorious.

Afterwards, Coach Tanzino felt confident that his team was ready for the first match that was only four days away. His wrestlers were putting in countless hours of hard work and dedicating themselves to the lifestyle needed to be a top notch athlete. They were all watching their weight and working extra as needed to get to their desired weight class.

Vincent knew that weighing in on a regular basis was a difficult task if done the wrong way, which is why he taught his athletes about the benefits of a proper diet, versus dropping a bunch of weight in a short period of time. He knew the health risks involved with cutting weight, and didn't want any of his athletes to have any adverse problems or fail to maintain their weight and in-turn hurt themselves or the team.

Besides, he felt that this was another learning tool, as many of his athletes had never really understood the value of what they consumed. Nutrition was an extremely important aspect of wrestling and Vincent felt as though by educating them, he was giving his athletes another advantage over their opponents. He also recognized that he was teaching them lessons beyond the wrestling mat, as it became another opportunity to teach his athletes valuable skills that they'd benefit from well beyond their time as a wrestler.

Chapter Ten

The Parkside Mustangs
– VS –
The East High Eagles

Tuesday: November 18th, 2014

All of the hard work and dedication over the past few weeks would be put to the test as the first match of the season was upon the Parkside Mustangs. The team was starting the season off with the East High Eagles, the reigning Big Eight Conference Champions and one of Parkside's four dual team losses from the previous season. Most teams wouldn't schedule such a formidable opponent right off the bat, but Coach Tanzino wanted to test his wrestlers every chance he could as he knew that this was the best way to prepare them for greater success throughout the entire season. The East High Eagles were ranked eighth in the states 4A Division, which also had Parkside slotted four spots behind them.

The Parkside Mustangs arrived at the East High Eagles gym ready for the battle that would ensue against an opponent that was a championship contender. The night that the Eagles defeated the Mustangs during the previous seasons' state dual team tournament was the same night that Vincent set this match up. Coach knew that the only way to earn the respect of others was to continuously challenge the best teams the state had to offer.

After arriving and getting organized in the visitors' locker room, the weigh-ins was set to begin. Both teams stood in the Eagles' locker room, as the Mustangs remained quiet, since Coach Tanzino liked to see his athletes focused from the onset of the match, which to him, began at weigh-ins. Comparatively, a couple of the East High Eagles wrestlers were joking around. To Vincent, he felt as though those wrestlers weren't taking it serious enough and lacked restraint, but it wasn't his problem, as his athletes knew what was expected of them.

The Mustangs took their turns stepping onto the scale. Each wrestler took the opportunity to check out who they'd likely be facing in their upcoming match, giving themselves a chance to mentally prepare for what was to come. As expected, everyone made weight, as they knew that they didn't want to disappoint their teammates or their coach. Each wrestler knew just how important it was to be on weight to give the team a chance to win the match. Besides, this was just another way to show how dedicated they were to their team and at achieving their goals.

Afterwards, the Mustangs went back to their locker room. Each wrestler got dressed and ate the meal that was prepared for them; nothing fattening, just some carbohydrates, fruit, and Gatorade to rehydrate and provide each and every one of them with enough energy to wrestle their match and come away victorious. The team wore their silver and Carolina blue warm-ups with matching t-shirts and shorts underneath. They also put on the teams regular singlets, which were Carolina blue with a white Mustang across the front and Parkside written in silver letters on the left leg.

The Mustangs saying for the year, "Expect the Unexpected," was located on the back of the t-shirts. This mantra was there to represent the team believing that they'd do better than people had planned for them to as well as Coach T's coaching style. He was a master of changing and maneuvering his lineup to adapt to their opponent or any given situation. Vincent believed that by adapting, it provided the Mustangs with the best opportunity to win each and every match. This sometimes meant that a backup could be placed in the started lineup and a starter moved to a different weight class.

Sometimes this would cause one or more of the starters to not wrestle a match, even if they were supposed to. However, everyone understood that this was just an aspect of the teamwork that they had dedicated themselves to and ultimately was what was best for the team. Nobody ever questioned Coach Tanzino's ways, as it had been proven to work. He studied a lot of film and scouted his opponents well enough to learn their strengths and weaknesses. Coupled with his in-depth knowledge of his own athletes, it gave him a distinct advantage in shifting his lineup around.

When it was time for the Mustangs to warm-up, they were led by their captains, Anthony Williams and Tim Ridley. For the next 10 minutes, they completed a variety of exercises before drilling a number of moves and then stretching, which was all focused on warming up their bodies and loosening up their muscles. Afterwards, the team moved to the center of the mat, forming a circle, in order to say a prayer together.

After the Mustangs had finished, they went behind the bench for a quick meeting with Coach Tanzino. As the team formed a half circle around Coach, the lights dimmed until they were all out, except for a spotlight that was focused on the center of the mat. Music began to play and the East High Eagles ran onto the mat for their turn to warm-up. The enthusiastic East High crowd roared as they cheered on the home team in this highly anticipated season opener.

Coach Tanzino, ignored what was going on around him, as he began speaking to the team, "Forget about the lights, the music, and the crowd. This is what we've been training hard for. This is the team that knocked us out of the dual team championships last year and I want to get even. This match sets the pace for the season. There are a lot of people watching to see who comes out of this the winner and I know that will be us! We're the new standard of excellence in North Carolina and the sooner we realize it, the sooner each of us can do our part to make it happen. It hasn't been an easy road, many of you have bumps and bruises already and we haven't even seen an opponent yet, but that's the name of the game. We need to be physically tough, but more importantly mentally tough. You need to believe that you can win, because if you don't believe that, then you won't win, and you have no business stepping onto the mat tonight or any other night."

The entire team intently listened to every word Coach Tanzino said and each of them understood what was required of them to win. They knew that each and every time they stepped onto the mat it would be a dog fight and they needed to be prepared to dig deep down into their soul and will themselves to victory. Each and every wrestler nodded to show Coach that they understood and were completely prepared to go out onto the mat and show everyone what they were made of.

"Is there anything that anyone would like to add," Vincent stated as he waited to see if there was a response, but there wasn't, "alright gentlemen, it's time to show everyone that the Mustangs have arrived. Mustangs on three: one, two, three!"

"Mustangs!" was emphatically cheered in unison as the team was ready for anything that the Eagles would throw at them.

As the match began, Anthony remained behind the bench warming up. He kept his sweat going while cheering on his teammates. As the dual meet progressed, it was clear to everyone that each match was going to play a significant role in this battle of championship caliber teams. The highly ranked East High Eagles were being challenged on their home mat by the underdog Parkside Mustangs. But in the eyes of the Mustangs, they knew that they were the better squad and undeniably the team to beat.

The battle began with Parkside's 126 and 132 pound wrestlers earning decisions, providing their team with a 6-0 lead in the dual meet. However, the lead didn't last long as the next three matches went to the East High Eagles, giving them a 9-6 advantage. But the Eagles lead would be highly contested as the Parkside Mustangs began their assault on the middle of the lineup.

The next wrestler to have a chance at the Eagles was Anthony. He had been watching the first five matches, while warming up, and saw many of the tendencies that Coach Tanzino had warned his team about. They were predictable with the moves that they used, which he felt would help the rest of his team, because they had prepared to defend them while in practice. But before the rest of the Mustangs had a chance to showcase their talents, Anthony knew he'd have to set the pace for the rest of his teammates and pin his opponent quickly.

Vincent approached Anthony as he was finishing his warm-up. A warm-up that gave Anthony just the right amount of sweat, but without making him too tired for his match. It was an important balance between loosening up his muscles and preparing his lunges for the match; yet, not exerting too much energy that would cause him to be flat or drained. But Anthony had perfected this balance over the previous three seasons and the many off-season tournaments. He was a well-oil machine, ready to grind out a victory.

"First match of the year, are you excited?" questioned Coach Tanzino.

"I can hardly contain myself. This is my year to dominate everyone in my path for a state championship!" exclaimed Anthony.

"I know it is, but just remember to be smart out there. You set the pace, but nothing foolish. You're better than anyone you'll face this year, always know that and show that to the fans. Win with grace and style all at the same time."

"I will Coach," assured Anthony.

"Good. We're down by three, I need you to show your dominance and get a good match in before you pin him. I need 6 team points out of you."

"I'll get at least a 10 point lead and then pin him."

"Perfect. Now go out there and show everyone how prepared you are for an unforgettable senior season." Coach Tanzino gave Anthony a smack on the butt as he darted through the tunnel formed by his teammates and onto the mat.

Anthony made it to the center of the mat where the referee and his opponent were already standing. He took one look into the eyes of his opponent and saw fear. Instantly, he knew that he had already won the match, and the whistle hadn't even blown yet.

As they shook hands and the whistle was blown by the official, Anthony immediately went on the offensive. He took control of an inside tie up, placing his right hand on the back of his opponents neck and his left on the inside of his shoulder. This gave Anthony control of the East High wrestler, which he quickly benefited from. Anthony pulled down on his opponents head, and as the wrestler lifted his head up, Anthony effortlessly took a high crotch shot and immediately switched to a double leg takedown. His opponent didn't even know what had hit him as he was on the ground, having given up two points for the takedown and was already on his back. Anthony held him down for a five count before he let him roll himself to his stomach. With a three point near fall, Anthony was now up 5-0 and the match wasn't even 15 seconds old.

Anthony instinctively began working for more points. He wanted to turn his opponent two more times before he'd finally pin him and put him out of his misery. Anthony used his right hand to take hold of his opponents left wrist, which was tucked close to his stomach, before sinking in a bar arm. Anthony wanted to gain a quick set of back points as he used the bar arm to get a cheap tilt, earning him three more points and an 8-0 advantage. As Anthony let his opponent get back to his stomach, he released his arm to work on riding legs. He quickly wrapped his left leg around his opponent's left leg, giving him complete control over his opponent's lower extremity. Anthony cocked his right leg back and with all of his force, threw his body to the other side of his opponent, twisting the East High wrestler up as Anthony grabbed hold of his face for a Jacob's hook; where he gained three more near fall points and increased his lead to 11-0.

As Anthony let his opponent get back to his stomach, he could hear Coach yelling that it was time to finish the match. The team needed 6 team points for the pin, not 5 points for the technical pin, which he'd earn if he increased his lead to 15 or more points over his opponent. Anthony decided that it was time for one of his favorite moves, the hammer lock. As he situated his opponent, to be flat on his stomach, Anthony wrenched the kids left arm behind his back, then sunk his left arm under his opponents' right armpit and grabbed hold of his left wrist, which was situated snuggly against his own back. Once he had it locked in, Anthony knew that the match was all but over. Anthony ran his body clockwise towards the head with the hammer lock securely fastened and easily forced his opponent to his back, all while Anthony grabbed hold of his opponents' head with a reverse half. The referee got down close, silently counted two and blew his whistle as he slapped the mat indicating a pin had been earned by Anthony. The combatants stood up in the center of the mat where they shook hands prior to the official raising Anthony's arm showing to the crowd that he was indeed victorious. It only took Anthony a minute to dispense of his opponent, but a minute that clearly solidified Anthony's complete and utter dominance.

The roar of the crowd, which was a mixture of cheers from the Mustang faithful and boos from the home crowd, greeted Anthony as he jogged off the mat and slapped Vincent's hand. A smile ran across his face as he had notched his first victory of the season. Now that his turn on the mat was over, it was time for him to throw his sweats back on, and continue to help cheer on his teammates, while giving them hints on moves to watch out for or that they could use throughout the remainder of the tightly contested competition.

The Parkside Mustangs now had a 12-9 lead over the Eagles, but half of the dual meet still remained. Tim was up next and quickly earned a pin to keep the ball rolling for the Mustangs. After Tim's match, Parkside continued to show their dominance as they went on to earn five victories out the last seven matches, bringing with it a 36–18 win, which solidified the fact that they were going to be a force to be reckoned with in North Carolina throughout the season. This also gave them a chance to jump up in the state rankings as they had defeated an elite caliber team, while proudly avenging a loss from the previous season. The victory also provided Vincent with his first career win against the East High Eagles, a team that was consistently amongst the upper echelon in the state.

Once the match was over, both teams lined up to walk across the mat and shake hands with each other. The East High Eagles were visibly upset with the loss, while the Parkside Mustangs were filled with satisfaction. The last people to shake hands were the opposing coaches. Coach Tanzino was congratulated on a great victory, while Vincent wished the East High Eagles good luck on the upcoming season. Vincent knew that they'd likely meet up again at some point throughout the season, especially in the state duals, but he liked his chances in obtaining the same result in a rematch.

After shaking hands, the Mustangs met behind the bench, as was customary, to allow the smiling Coach Tanzino to go over his thoughts on the dual meet. "I don't have a lot to say tonight fella's besides great first match of the year! There's a lot more of that to come as long as we remain focused on the ultimate prize, a state championship!"

The team cheered in unison, as they were ecstatic for what they had just accomplished and how happy coach was with them.

The smiling wrestlers immediately began to grab their belongings and the team's equipment. Everyone mingled, for a few minutes, with their families and friends who had made the trip to support them, before walking out of the gym to head towards the bus for their 45 minute ride back to Parkside High School. A ride that they'd enjoy as traveling always seemed better after a victory.

While everyone was leaving the gym, Anthony approached Coach Tanzino and asked, "Coach, can we sit and watch the match on the way back to the school?"

"That's fine by me as long as your parents don't want you to ride home with them," replied Vincent, as he had grown accustomed to this occurring.

Anthony promptly turned to his parents, who were standing next to him, "Mom, Dad, can I ride back on the bus so I can watch the film?"

A smiling Terrance Williams looked at his wife, Olivia, before answering, "That's fine."

"Thanks Dad. I love you guys. I'll see you at the school."

"We love you too," replied Olivia as she gave Anthony a hug and a kiss.

"Great match tonight," stated Terrance as he hugged Anthony.

"Thanks Dad," replied Anthony. He was visibly excited about the dominant performance that he'd just put on and the praise that he received from his parents. Everything that he had done was made possible by their sacrifices and he wanted nothing more than to honor them in every way imaginable.

As Anthony walked towards the bus with Coach Tanzino, he turned around, smiled and waved at his parents, who were visibly proud of the young man they had raised. They knew that all of the sacrifices they'd made over the years were paying huge dividends as they watched their son grow into a young man who was one of the country's elite and highly touted high school wrestlers. They were ready for what was to come that season, as they were confident that their son would be rewarded with a state championship for all of his efforts.

Chapter Eleven

The Ride Home: 1-0

Tuesday: November 18[th,] 2014

The bus hadn't even departed from the East High parking lot by the time Anthony had grabbed the video camera to get it ready to start studying the film. Before Vincent had taken care of his coaching duties, by making sure that everyone was present and accounted for, Anthony already had the video set on the first match of the evening. Anthony sat patiently, intent on helping Coach discover ways in which the team could improve before the first tournament of the season on Saturday.

Once Vincent had gotten there, he hadn't even settled down into his set before Anthony pressed play. The two sat focused on the little screen, taking notes and discussing adjustments that each wrestler and the team as a whole needed to focus on. They spent the entire 45 minute trip dissecting the mistakes and coming up with solutions to fix the problems as well as pointing out many of the positives from each bout. They were extremely satisfied to see more positives than negatives, even in the bouts that they lost, as everyone had fought hard and given it their all.

Coach Tanzino enjoyed this time with Anthony as it was a way to expand Anthony's wrestling knowledge, while grooming him for his future, which he was sure would include coaching. Besides, they had a special bond, like brothers or even Vincent being like a second father figure to Anthony. Vincent had grown extremely close to Anthony and his parents and he wanted to impart all of his knowledge to him so that he had the ability to accomplish all of his dreams.

It was apparent to Coach Tanzino that Anthony had an uncanny knack for grasping new concepts and being able to teach those techniques to others. Anthony had grown into an additional assistant coach for Vincent and an athlete that he'd severely miss after the season was over and had moved on to college. Vincent had intentions of watching Anthony wrestle collegiately whenever possible, along with going to visit him wherever he ended up, even if it wasn't at West Virginia University.

For a few moments, Vincent sat back with a huge smile on his face and just enjoyed listening to Anthony figure out the next step for the team. He was amazed and proud of how mature of a young man Anthony had become. He was more than just an athlete, he was family and Vincent was honored to have played any part in helping Anthony develop into the person that he had become.

As the team arrived at Parkside, they were greeted by cheers from the friends and family members that were awaiting their return. There was a buzz in the air that was filled with excitement and anticipation for the upcoming season. One by one, the wrestlers and their families left, leaving Anthony and Coach Tanzino to be the only ones waiting in the parking lot. Each was in an extremely happy mood as they discussed the growth that the team had made over the past eight months to be at this point, taking down a powerhouse like East High.

They talked about what was coming next in the training regimen so that the team would continue to grow instead of just being satisfied or become complacent due to this tremendous win to start off the season. They discussed ways that Anthony could assist the team in the coming months as they both had a deep desire to achieve their goal of a state championship campaign. All in all, they sat there talking for a long period of time, not even noticing that an hour had passed, yet, the Williams' never showed up.

Vincent reached into his pocket as his phone began to ring. The picture, name, and number for Bill Robbins popped up on his screen. Bill was a police officer who Vincent had gotten to know from the many times he worked security at a number of the Parkside sporting events. Vincent assumed he had already heard the big news of their victory that evening and was calling to congratulate him. Vincent took a few steps away from Anthony and answered the call, "Hey Bill, how are things going?"

"Well, they've been better. Are you with Anthony?" questioned Bill.

"Yeah, why, what's going on?" wondered Vincent as this caught him off guard.

In a sad tone, Officer Robbins responded, "There's been an accident. It's the Williams'."

Vincent immediately became concerned as he heard their name, "What happened? Are they alright?"

Unsure how to proceed with the news, Officer Robbins replied, "A drunk driver hit them head on over by the Park. I'm sorry Vincent, but they're already dead."

Shock covered Vincent's face as he just realized his friends were dead and that he'd be forced to break the news to Anthony; news that he wasn't prepared to tell one of his wrestlers, especially one that he'd grown so close to. Without thinking twice he told Bill that they'd be right over to the Park. But, before Officer Robbins could respond to tell him otherwise, Vincent ended the call. As he turned around to face Anthony, Vincent noticed an inquisitive look on his face. Coach Tanzino slowly walked back to where Anthony was standing with a confused look on his face.

"Coach, what's wrong, what happened? Is it Vanessa?" questioned Anthony.

Vincent put his hands on Anthony's shoulders as he began to divulge the horrible news. "No Anthony, it's not Vanessa, it's your parents."

"Why? What happened?"

"They were in a car accident. They were in the Park on their way here and were hit head on by a drunk driver."

"Are they okay? Are they in the hospital?" wondered Anthony. Anthony's once happy and excited mood quickly changed to one of concern and confusion.

Vincent took a deep breath and in a caring and loving voice he said words that he never anticipated ever having to say, "Anthony, they're dead."

Anthony stood for a few moments in shock before emphatically yelling, "No, it can't be! It can't be true!"

With an intense sense of sorrow, Vincent responded, "Unfortunately it is. I'm so sorry Anthony."

Anthony broke down into tears as he dropped to the ground. It was as if he had no control over his motor skills. Vincent sat down next to him and put his arms around Anthony to embrace him. Anthony sat there crying in Vincent's arms for what seemed like an eternity to him. So numb and shocked from the news that his parents had died. Guilt encompassed Anthony as he felt as though it was somehow his fault. Anthony thought to himself how they wouldn't have been near the park tonight had he just gone home with them instead of riding on the bus with Coach and the rest of his teammates. Or if he never had been wrestling at all, then they'd still be alive. But Anthony never said a word, he just cried as Vincent held onto him.

For the next 20 minutes, Vincent let Anthony cry in his arms before he picked him up and helped him into his Jeep. As they drove to the Park, Anthony stared out the window, not saying a word as tears streamed down his cheeks.

The police had blocked off part of the road to prevent anyone from being near the accident while they waited for the coroner to come and pick up the bodies. This prevented Vincent from driving to the wreckage, but as he stopped a half mile down the road, Anthony jumped out of the vehicle and began running towards the police cars and the site of the accident. Before Anthony could get to his parents, he was stopped by Officer Robbins. Bill knew this was a scene that Anthony shouldn't see. Vincent quickly caught up to them and helped restrain Anthony.

As they sat there, Bill described the events that led to the accident and what he believed had transpired. Bill told them that the drunk driver hit Terrance and Olivia head on, instantly killing them as the impact caused the vehicle to slam into some trees. The woman had minor wounds and was taken to the hospital for her injuries along with testing her blood-alcohol level. After discovering she had a blood alcohol level twice the legal limit, they arrested her for Vehicular Manslaughter. They discovered an empty bottle of vodka in her car, which had sustained damage, but nothing compared to the Williams' vehicle.

It was all so surreal. Only a couple of hours earlier they were alive and so proud of their sons' accomplishments. But now, everything had changed in an instant. Two amazing people had lost their lives due to the irreconcilable actions of a woman who couldn't control her drinking habits.

Officer Robbins encouraged them to go home, as there was nothing that they could do there. Especially since he felt that it wasn't a situation that Anthony should be subjected to. Bill didn't want Anthony to be there when the bodies were taken away as he felt that it could be too much for the young man. Vincent listened to Bill's advice and he brought Anthony back to his Jeep.

Vincent didn't know what to do with Anthony after they left the park. Unsure of how to handle it all, Vincent picked up the phone and called the only person that he knew could help him sort all of this out, Vanessa. He told her about the accident, the call he received from Bill Robbins, and how he had to break the news to Anthony. While Vincent talked to Vanessa, Anthony sat there oblivious to his surroundings as he concentrated on the pain and the anguish of his current predicament.

Vanessa told Vincent that he should bring Anthony home with him and that she'd meet them at his place to help out. Vincent was happy that she'd be there because he didn't think he could handle all of this on his own. He hadn't even taken a moment to mourn the loss of two of his closest friends, because he needed to be strong and supportive for Anthony.

Even though it only took a few minutes to get to Vincent's place, Vanessa was already inside by the time they got there. She had the spare room set up for Anthony and some food in case they were hungry, but neither could eat. Anthony went right to the spare room and locked himself in. This gave Vincent time to let out his emotions while Vanessa held onto him. All Vincent could think about was Anthony and how unfair this tragedy was. As an educator and a coach, nothing prepared him for a situation like this. But he was more than just a coach to them, he was family. They were his best friends and they were gone, leaving Anthony all alone. Vincent continued to cry, as Vanessa comforted him. He didn't know what to do next. All he knew was that he had to be there for Anthony in any way possible. Vincent realized that right now was his only chance to let out his emotions, because from here on out, he needed to be strong because everything would be about Anthony and what he had lost.

Chapter Twelve

The Funeral

Saturday: November 22nd, 2014

Saturday, November 22nd was another otherwise beautiful and mild fall afternoon, a factor which under other circumstances had brought so many people to the Charlotte area. Many of them hailed from the north and were vehemently trying to get away from the blistering winters, while others moved from various locations to have the experience of enjoying all four seasons. If it wasn't for the funeral, many of those in attendance would have relished this day, as they either watched College Football or participated in a wrestling tournament. But for one person in particular, this day was a tragic moment that would alter the rest of his life.

There was a lot that had to be done for the funeral, but Anthony was in no position to complete the arduous tasks. This left Vincent to take on the responsibility of finalizing all of the funeral arrangements so that the Williams' could be laid to rest. The Parkside wrestling team skipped their already scheduled tournament in order to be at the Williams' funeral as they wanted to support their friend throughout this difficult time.

As many friends arrived to the funeral, it was evident that Terrance and Olivia's families were absent as they continued to hold ill will towards them. Vincent even tried to reach out to any living relatives that he could locate, but other than one of Olivia's cousins, nobody seemed receptive. This bothered Vincent, but he wasn't surprised as he had heard many stories about them from Terrance and Olivia. But, that wasn't his main concern, as his focus was entirely on Anthony.

The room was filled with floral arrangements and sorrowful faces that focused on the caskets made of rich mahogany. As someone that the Williams' considered family, Vincent was willing to do whatever it took to aid his deceased friends; who had only been gone for a few days and were already sorely missed. Anthony had remained at Vincent's since the accident, barely even leaving the room for any reason. This caused Vincent to go to the Williams' residence to grab Sammie along with some clothes and other belongings that Anthony needed as he didn't want to go back to his house without his parents.

Vincent and Vanessa were being as supportive as possible to Anthony, who had become a bit of a recluse ever since the tragedy occurred. He hadn't been at school, practice, or even talked to any of his friends since Tuesday night because he couldn't handle talking about anything that was going on. The only person that seemed to get anything out of him was Amanda, but it wasn't much at all.

As everyone sat at the funeral home, facing the front of the room, gazing at Terrance and Olivia's caskets, Vincent stood up to say a few words for the friends that he had just lost and the parents of a promising young man who he had been fortunate enough to get to know very well.

"I've known Terrance and Olivia Williams for a few years, ever since Anthony started wrestling. Their love and undying devotion to one another is something that everyone should strive to have for themselves. But, their biggest accomplishment in life was their son Anthony as he meant the world to them. Everything that they've done was for his benefit and I'm truly sorry for his loss. Terrance and Olivia Williams have left us way too soon. May God be with them and their memories live on with all of us."

As Vincent sat back down, one by one, people began to file out of the funeral home. They said their final goodbyes as they walked out and headed to their cars to make their way to the cemetery. Anthony, Vincent, Vanessa, Amanda and the six pallbearers remained behind to have a few minutes alone with Terrance and Olivia Williams. As the caskets were closed, tears streamed down the faces of almost everyone sitting in the room. However, Vincent didn't cry, even though he wanted to, because he felt as though he had to remain strong for Anthony, who needed him now more than ever.

Since their families were not present, six of Anthony's teammates and friends were asked to carry the caskets. The Pallbearers consisted of four wrestlers, Tim Ridley, Chris States, Mike Robinson, and Ryan Thompson along with Al Nelson their assistant coach and Anthony's friend Ben Bradley.

They carried the caskets one at a time out of the funeral home and into the two Hearst's for their trip to the cemetery and their final resting place. The six pallbearers road in one of the limo's, while Vincent, Vanessa, Amanda and Anthony road in the other. Amanda held Anthony's hand the entire time as she didn't have any words to say that could help, but she wanted to show her devotion and support for the guy she loved.

While Vincent remained strong for everyone, Vanessa continuously teared up because of the heartache that was present all around her. Her sadness overwhelmed her at one point as she turned away from Anthony while the tears flowed freely. She felt that he didn't need to see how emotionally affected she was by all of this. Vincent noticed this and embraced Vanessa, holding her close, as he showed how much he loved her and was there for her throughout this trying time.

Once the caskets were in place and the funeral precession were all present at the cemetery, the priest stood in front of everyone to say some final words and prayers before the caskets would be lowered into the ground. Vincent and Vanessa stood to the left of Anthony, while Amanda was on his right holding his hand as she placed her head on his shoulder. This caused the tears that were streaming down her face to make a puddle on his jacket, but Anthony didn't even notice as he appeared to be oblivious to the world around him. His usually happy disposition was filled with emptiness and a sense of hopelessness. Anthony had lost the most important people in his life, and he felt as though he was the reason that they were dead. He didn't know what to do or what to think as he felt as though he was all alone, in-spite of the support he had from everyone.

The priest began to give his sermon, "We are gathered here today to pay our final respects to these two wonderful members of God's flock. Terrance and Olivia Williams lived their lives for two purposes, to bring joy and happiness into the hearts of everyone they came in contact with and to provide for their son Anthony.

"I have had many conversations with them about how proud they were of him. They talked about all of his athletic accomplishments, but were even happier with his academic successes. Their entire world revolved around the one thing that brought them more joy than anything else, their son. And for him, I am deeply sorry for his loss. It's never easy to lose a loved one, especially at such a young age.

"Even though their physical presence will no longer be seen on this earth, their spirit lives on forever in the minds and hearts of everyone that's here today. We were all touched by them and we have all suffered a great loss in our lives. But, we must always know that they have left a legacy that lives on through Anthony and that they are now in a better place."

The priest continued, "Let us pray," as everyone in unison, but Anthony, recited "The Our Father Prayer."

After the ceremony, everyone took a few moments to have one last look at the caskets before heading back to their vehicles and on with their lives. Once most of the congregation had left, the caskets began to be lowered to their final resting place. When they made it to the bottom of the grave, Vanessa and Amanda walked back to the limo, leaving Vincent and Anthony alone.

Vincent wanted to give Anthony as much time as he needed while looking one last time at the caskets that housed his parents. Tears trickled down Anthony's face, as he wasn't able to prevent them from happening, even though he wanted them to stop. He didn't want anyone to see his true emotions, not even Coach Tanzino. All he wanted to do was bottle up his feelings and emotions as he never wanted to experience pain like this ever again. At all costs, he was determined to never be hurt again.

A few moments after the caskets had made it to their final resting place, Anthony and Vincent watched as two men shoveled dirt on top of them. There was no way of stopping it now, as these were the final fleeting moments with his parents. Little by little, the dirt began to cover up the caskets, as Anthony thought about how they'd never be seen again or their inhabitants.

Chapter Thirteen

Reading of the Will

Monday: November 24, 2014

Anthony and Vincent missed school on Monday, November 24, to meet with the Williams' family attorney and discuss their Will as a number of things needed to be taken care of. Anthony really hadn't spoken very much to anyone up to this point as he was still in a state of shock. He remained at Vincent's house as neither Vincent nor Vanessa allowed Anthony to be alone in such a difficult time in his life. Besides, he really didn't have anywhere else to go. They were as supportive as possible, in-spite of the fact that Anthony didn't want anything from anyone. All he wanted was to be left alone. He wasn't taking or returning phone calls or texts and was barely eating as he basically had become a hermit. However, Vincent forced Anthony to get ready and take a ride with him today to see the Williams' attorney.

They arrived a few minutes early for their 10 am appointment with, Mr. Steven Rice. As they entered his law offices, they were greeted by a friendly, young, and beautiful receptionist who tried to be friendly with Anthony, but he just ignored her. It didn't seem to bother her as she was well aware of the circumstances for this visit. She felt sorry for Anthony as she had met and liked his parents.

As Vincent and Anthony walked into Steven's office, he greeted them with a smile and a firm handshake. Steven Rice was dressed in a nice grey suit, which didn't do anything to hide the extra weight that he carried, which was mostly due to him sitting for hours on end behind his desk working on cases or completing paperwork as well as the fact that he enjoyed his food. Nonetheless, he was a very jolly and pleasant man who had been practicing law for over 20 years.

Steven immediately apologized for having to meet under the current circumstances and quickly began to speak about Terrance and Olivia's Will. Vincent seemed to be the only one paying attention or reacting to what was going on as Anthony remained distant throughout the entire meeting, almost as if he didn't hear anything that was said by the lawyer or Vincent. He just sat in one of the plush leather chairs, across from the attorney, staring out the window. He wasn't looking at anything in particular, he just didn't want to be there dealing with the finality of his parents' estate.

Steven didn't waste any time getting down to business, as he always found that to be the best method, instead of having a bunch of small talk during a time like this. "Vincent, you're the executor of the Williams' Estate. You and Anthony are the only two people mentioned in the Will. Since the Williams' had no living relatives or at least ones that they had any contact with, they thought that you'd be the best person to fulfill their last wishes," stated Mr. Rice.

"Of course," replied Vincent as he expected that he might have something to do with taking care of everything, or at least helping Anthony do so.

Mr. Rice continued, "Vincent, this isn't going to be easy. Terrance and Olivia's financial situation wasn't ideal. They were over-extended on the house and some of their assets are tied up for a period of time. With that being said, they have requested that you sell the house, the furniture, the boat, and the cars in order to pay off all of their debts. With the remaining money, they'd like for you to set up a trust fund for Anthony. They'd like for him to get half to use once he turns 18 so that he can pay for college and the remainder to be available to him once he graduates from whatever university he chooses. They've also left you some money to take care of their biggest request."

"Which is?" inquired Vincent.

The words resonated loudly for Vincent as he heard them uttered by Steven, "They left you as Anthony's guardian."

Vincent turned his gaze to Anthony, who sat there with a distant look on his face, not even reacting to anything that had just been stated. Vincent realized the gravity of this request. He had a feeling that would be the case due to the lack of family, but until he heard the words, it really hadn't sunk in yet. As Vincent got up and walked over to Anthony to give him a hug, tears began to stream down Anthony's face. Even though it appeared as though he wasn't paying attention, indeed he was, and he knew that his life would never be the same again. His parents were gone and so was the place that he called home.

As he hugged Anthony, Vincent replied, "I'd be honored to take care of Anthony, he's family to me. Is there anything else that needs to be taken care of?"

"A number of state agencies will be in contact with you in regards to your taking over guardianship of Anthony. I have a list of their substantial debts and have a number for a realtor that can help you expedite the process of selling everything. Mr. Tanzino, this will take some time and a lot of effort on your part to get all of this taken care of. If you need anything from me or some names of people to help you set everything up, I would be happy to assist."

"Thank you, I appreciate it," replied Vincent.

"Know this, I was sad to hear the news, the Williams' were a wonderful couple. I've known Terrance quite a few years and know that you're the right man for the job to take care of Anthony. They held you in high regards and always told me such wonderful things about the man that had become family to them. They trusted you with their most valuable asset as they believed that you could help him grow up to be the best man possible."

"They meant the world to me and so does Anthony. I'll do anything in my power to provide for him and to make this difficult time as easy as possible."

They completed some paperwork that was necessary to take care of the Williams' wishes. Once Vincent had signed all of the documents, he thanked Mr. Rice for his assistance and grabbed Anthony. They headed out of the office and over to the Williams' house, which was the first time that Anthony had stepped foot back into it without his parents. Vincent had gone over twice to grab clothes for Anthony and a number of other items that were needed for the funeral, but Anthony had refused to go with him. This time, he nodded his head in agreement as Vincent asked if he'd like to go to his home while they were out of school that day. Vincent figured that it might be a good idea, when it was just the two of them, to begin gathering the rest of Anthony's belonging to take over to Vincent's house.

They also needed to start planning what to sell and how to sell the various items. Vincent wanted to store anything that Anthony felt he might want later in life. But everything that Anthony was asked about, he just said "No," that he didn't want anything that might remind him of his parents. Vincent knew that he'd regret that decision once he got over the loss of his parents and without telling Anthony, he began to plan what items he'd place in a storage unit for him to have once he'd recovered from the traumatic loss and old enough to respect the fact that he had a number of his parents' possessions.

Vincent planned to store pictures, some of the furniture and a few personal items the he knew Anthony would want. He also planned to discuss with Vanessa what she felt that Anthony might want to hold onto so that he didn't miss anything. This was a major responsibility that had been placed onto Vincent's lap, enough so that he knew that he needed substantial help from Vanessa and others. But, no matter how much work was needed, Vincent was more than willing to do anything necessary so that Anthony didn't have to. Vincent's main focus was Anthony, as he attempted to make the best of this horrible situation.

Chapter Fourteen

The Move

Sunday: November 30th, 2014

Half of the Parkside wrestling team met at the Williams' residence early Sunday morning to help pack everything up and officially move Anthony in with Vincent. They loaded up the U-Haul Truck with the items that Vincent planned to save and store for Anthony, while many of the other items were loaded into a separate truck to be brought to the places that had already purchased them.

Anthony didn't talk much or interact with the others as he mostly wandered throughout the house or sat on the back deck looking at the lake. It was as if he was remembering all of the good times that he had with his parents and enjoying one last day in the place that he'd no longer be able to call home. The house hadn't even been on the market for more than a couple of days and there were already a number of interested buyers. The real estate agent felt that they could move the home and take care of any outstanding debt within the month, which is why they were moving everything out of the residence so soon after the funeral.

This definitely took some of the pressure off of Vincent's shoulders as things were moving along quickly and without any difficulties. He knew that the quicker they took care of it all, the sooner Anthony's future could be set and he could return to as normal of a life as possible. Everyone diligently worked and within a few hours, everything had been moved to its new home.

Once Vincent and Anthony finally had everything at his residence and everyone had left, Anthony finally spoke to Vincent about what was on his mind. He was going to quit the wrestling team as he believed it was the lone reason that his parents were dead. Anthony knew that the only reason they were driving through the park that night was because they were supporting him and his foolish dreams. He strongly believed that if he hadn't been wrestling, then they'd still be alive today. Besides, the sport just wasn't a priority for him anymore. He had dedicated so much time and effort to make his parents proud of him and earn a scholarship so that they didn't have to pay for his college education, an education that he wasn't sure he wanted, because now that they were gone, none of that mattered to him anymore.

Without giving Vincent any further details or even an opportunity to respond, Anthony went to his room, shut his door and locked himself in. Vincent heard the television turn on as he walked into his bedroom where Vanessa was.

Vincent joined Vanessa who was already sitting in bed, as it had been a long day of moving. The exhaustion was clearly evident on Vincent's face, even more than normal for this time of year. Vanessa was thoroughly worried about his well-being and what she could do to help him out. She knew how difficult this situation had been on Anthony, but not many people were even thinking about how Vincent was handling it all.

"Vincent, what are you going to do about everything? How are you going to handle raising Anthony, helping him cope with the loss of his parents, and selling their house while still maintaining everything at work?" questioned Vanessa as she was clearly concerned for the man that she loved.

"I'm going to do everything I can. I'll be here to help him return to as normal of a life as possible. I know that it may take time, but I'm going to be here every step of the way. I'm also not going to push the issue of him wrestling. If he chooses to return, then I'll welcome him back with open arms. Until then, I'll just try to ease his pain."

"Do you plan to do all of this alone?"

"I was hoping that you'd help me out. I could really use it. I'm sure he's not always going to want to talk to me, especially since I've been so close to his parents for the last few years and might remind him of them. I know a woman's touch is needed."

Vanessa touched Vincent's hand, "I'm not going anywhere. Of course I'll help. I was already planning on it."

"Thanks babe, I'm going to need you around even more," admitted Vincent.

Vanessa smiled as she asked, "Is this your way of asking me to move in?"

"Well, that wasn't what I meant, but it sounds like a great idea to me. I know that Anthony could use your help."

"Is that the only reason you want me to move in, to help Anthony?"

Vincent smirked, as he wanted her to move in for a long time now, just the right time hadn't come up for it to happen. But, with everything that was going on, he felt that this was the ideal time for it to occur. "No, by no means is that the case. I love you and want you to be in my life forever. This is for me as well. I've never raised a kid before. I'm scared that I'll mess up," confessed Vincent.

Vanessa loved Vincent and hated seeing him in this much pain. She had never seen him doubt himself before, but she knew that the stress of the entire situation had really taken its toll on him. "But you have! You've been raising athletes and students for years, ever since you graduated college and took this teaching and coaching job. You've been more of a parent to some of your athletes and students than their own parents. You're ready and will be an amazing parent," reassured Vanessa.

"I know. I was just planning that the first kid that I raised would be ours."

Vanessa was surprised, "Really? Were you going to clue me in on that plan?"

"Of course I was. I was hoping that we'd eventually get married and have kids. You're the only woman that I've truly loved and who completely understands me for who I am, a workaholic who takes my work home with me."

"And that's what I love about you. I know that you'll do anything it takes to be successful. And this won't be any different of a situation. You'll be fine and you'll make the right choices when it comes to Anthony."

"I hope so," stated Vincent as he grabbed Vanessa for a big embrace. He held her tight and gave Vanessa an intimate kiss. He wanted to show his appreciation for all of her support because he knew that without her, he didn't know how successful he'd be at handling everything that had been placed in his lap.

Teaching and coaching kids was one thing, but raising them was entirely different, especially under these circumstances. Vincent knew that he had experienced loss at a young age as his grandparents and other relatives had passed away, but he recognized that it was nothing compared to someone losing their parents. He just hoped that Anthony would eventually open up and talk to him about everything. Anthony was hurting and for the first time, Vincent wasn't sure he had the solution. Vincent only hoped that he'd find a way to ease his pain, as he knew that it would never fully go away.

Chapter Fifteen

The Spiral Begins

Friday: December 5th, 2014

It was a little past eight in the evening as Anthony finished getting ready for his night out. It was going to be the first time that he truly faced many of his friends since the accident, a fact that he was dreading, but something that he felt he could ignore or at least forget about with every drink he consumed. Before heading downstairs, Anthony threw on a pair of jeans and a tight t-shirt for the night. He also packed an overnight bag as he had no intentions of returning to Vincent's after the party.

Anthony walked into the living room as Vincent was in the middle of taking notes on the teams' last match, a blowout victory against the Lake Norman Lancers, in preparation for the following day's dual team tournament at River Valley High School. The tournament was going to be a great test for the Mustangs, as six of the ten teams were ranked in the top ten of their respective classifications in the state. It was another attempt at seeing what his team was made of. As Vincent made the schedule, he marked this tournament down as a key stepping stone for his athletes as a team. If the Mustangs could take first place at the River Valley Duals, Vincent was positive that they could win their conference and likely a state dual team championship.

Vincent enjoyed watching film as he felt that it was the best way to properly prepare his team and fix any mistakes they were making. He felt as if this gave him a second or even a third look at ways to aid his team in achieving their ultimate goal of a state championship, a goal that had taken a major blow once Anthony quit the team. He was replaced by sophomore Dante Adams, who was a talented athlete, but nowhere near Anthony's caliber on the mat.

However, Vincent was confident that Dante would win more matches than he lost, which was all he needed out of the developing athlete. But deep down, Vincent knew that it would take more work on his end to win dual meets as he was generally guaranteed six team points when Anthony was in the lineup, versus not knowing how many team points Dante would be able to earn or even if he'd end up losing a close match.

As Vincent heard Anthony approaching, he looked up from his notes. He immediately noticed that Anthony was carrying a bag with him, but he didn't know why. Instead of jumping to any conclusions, Vincent felt as though a civilized conversation was needed. Unfortunately, that would've been a first in recent days, as Anthony barely conversed with him anymore and when they did talk, it was more yelling by Anthony than anything else. "Are you still going to help me out at the tournament tomorrow?" asked Vincent.

Anthony was annoyed as he replied, "I don't know. I'm heading out right now."

"Where are you going?" questioned Vincent, as he hadn't given Anthony permission to go anywhere.

"Ben's house and I probably won't be back tonight," angrily responded Anthony. He hated having to tell Vincent, or anyone for that matter, what he was doing.

Vincent knew this meant that Anthony, and many of the other Parkside students, would be drinking this evening, because that's the only reason why anyone hung out at Ben's house on the weekend. "You know how I feel about you drinking. Besides, you need to take responsibility for your actions because if you tell me you're going to help out, you need to do so."

An undeniable rage engulfed Anthony. "Get off my back! You're not my father, you can't tell me what to do," yelled Anthony. He was irritated that Vincent was trying to keep up with his every move.

Vincent responded calmly as he knew yelling wouldn't help out the situation. "While you're living here and I'm responsible for you, what you do does concern me."

Anthony started to walk towards the door as he continued to disrespect Vincent, "It shouldn't, so just leave me alone."

"Anthony, don't leave while we're talking," stated Vincent, as he tried to do anything to reach Anthony and prevent him from making bad decisions.

But Anthony ignored Vincent's desire to talk and continued to open the door, "You're the one talking, not me. I don't need this shit! I'm out of here!"

Anthony walked out and proceeded to slam the door shut as he left the house. Vincent was dejected and angered with the lack of respect that Anthony now showed him, especially after all of the time that they'd spent together and how close they'd been. Vincent was hurt, but understood how difficult all of this must be on Anthony. One minute he's on top of the world and the next minute everything came crashing down on him. Vincent just hoped that Anthony would soon snap out of the funk that he was in; otherwise, it would be a long dark road that he'd have to pull himself out of.

Anthony walked to his car, opened the door, put the key in the ignition and sped off down the road towards Amanda's house. Anthony now had no respect for the law as he blasted his music, disregarded all speed limits, and did as he pleased on the road. His reckless actions not only put himself in danger, but all those who were on the road. But, he didn't care anymore. Even though he had done everything right, life had been unfair to him. So, he figured why shouldn't he do as he pleased, especially if there was always going to be a negative outcome in the long run.

Anthony had even given up on walking up to Amanda's door and talking to her parents; instead, he just pulled up to her driveway and honked the horn. As he impatiently honked his horn for the third time, Amanda finally appeared at the door. She was carrying an overnight bag as she quickly made her way down the driveway. As Amanda entered Anthony's car, he didn't even wait for her to put on her seatbelt prior to taking off for Ben's house.

"What took you so long to get out here?" questioned Anthony, as he recklessly drove threw her neighborhood.

"I was grabbing my things and trying to explain to my parents why you don't talk to them anymore," responded Amanda.

"What did you say?"

"That we were in a hurry."

"Good, as long as they leave me alone."

This upset Amanda, as her parents loved Anthony, "What's wrong? You love my parents and they love you."

Angry that he had to have this conversation, Anthony yelled at Amanda, "I don't want to deal with them or anyone! Everyone just treats me like a child. I'm an adult! Why can't they see that?"

"Everyone's just concerned, we all care about you," explained Amanda.

Anthony ignored her comment because he was tired of explaining himself. They sat in silence for a few minutes before Amanda broke the awkwardness, "By the way, how are things with Coach?" since she knew how poorly Anthony had been treating him.

"He's still trying to control my life. The only reason I'm there is because my parents made sure I couldn't have any money until I turned 18. When that happens, I'm out."

Amanda knew that Anthony was wrong about Coach and was disappointed with the way that he'd been treating him. They'd been so close before the accident, and now Anthony didn't want anything to do with him. "You should really try to be nice to him. He's made a lot of sacrifices for you to move in with him."

"Whatever, he's just in it for the money my parents gave him. He's barely even giving any of it to me."

Amanda tried to defend Coach Tanzino, as he was just looking out for Anthony's best interests. "He's just making sure you don't blow it all on worthless possessions."

Anthony retorted, "Like what?"

"What about the flat screen TV or the PS3?"

Completely aggravated that Amanda would even bring up what he's been buying with his parents' money, Anthony replied, "All necessary items."

Amanda adamantly stated, "No they weren't!"

"Yes they were, and stop pissing me off!" yelled Anthony; an action that he never would've done prior to his parents passing away, as they wouldn't find this acceptable treatment of a woman.

Amanda was upset with how she was being treated, but stayed calm, "I'm not. I'm just trying to talk to you."

"I don't like it, so stop."

They were close to pulling up to Ben's, and instead of continuing the argument, Amanda tried to calm him down and get him to be nice to all of their friends. "Okay, we're here anyways, so let's just try to have fun, and please Anthony, don't get too drunk. I feel like all you want to do is get into arguments with everyone and have sex with me."

"I love being with you, that's why I love having sex with you, and I don't fight all the time."

"Well, you used to not be like this at all."

"I don't care. I'm going to grab some drinks and enjoy myself. Join me if you want to." And with that, he ended the conversation without truly listening to what Amanda was trying to say. All that mattered to Anthony was that he could do whatever he wanted to, without any limitations or anyone breathing down his neck.

As they pulled up to Ben's house, Anthony slammed on the breaks, almost crashing into a parked car. He was completely reckless and inconsiderate of others. His soul focus was himself. Instantly, after turning off the car, he jumped out of the vehicle and walked towards the house with Amanda trailing behind him. Once they reached the front door, they were greeted with handshakes and alcohol from the partygoers who had already been drinking.

Ben had a variety of drinks at his house: beer, wine coolers, vodka, and rum. Ben was a smart businessman when it came to his parties. He always had someone remain sober to collect the keys from anyone that was drinking and drove to the party along with ten dollars from the guys and the discounted rate of five dollars for the ladies to gain unlimited access to the alcoholic beverages that were available. Ben usually made money on his parties, but most of the time it was put back into use when he bought alcohol for the next event that he held. Besides, Ben didn't really need the money, as his parents were extremely wealthy, but he still wasn't going to do all of this for free.

The surround sound stereo was bumping, the alcohol was flowing, and many patrons were partaking in various drinking games.

As Anthony and Amanda made their way through the living room and into the kitchen, they were sharply greeted with a group of half-naked teenagers, laughing and finishing a hand of strip poker.

Ben smiled as he continued to win, causing the females playing to keep undressing, "You lose again ladies. It's your turn to take off some clothes." This prompted every female at the table to take off an item of their choice. But by this point, there weren't many options, as everyone was nearly naked.

"You finally got me to my bra and panties Ben. This of course is the only way that would ever happen," laughed Brittany.

Josh, one of Ben's closest friends, who was also a senior at Parkside and a regular at his parties, was amused by this and quickly added, "Damn that sucks."

"Shut-up man," angrily stated Ben, "Brittany, that's not how I got you naked last weekend."

"Right, you got me wasted and took advantage of me," replied Brittany.

Ben defended himself, "No I didn't! You were very willing."

"Too bad it only lasted a minute," laughed Brittany.

"That's a lie!" exclaimed Ben.

"Nope, ask anyone that was there. Jackie isn't that how it went?" asked Brittany.

"It was like they didn't even leave the party," added Jackie, the beautiful brunette cheerleader that was sitting next to Brittany, and another regular at the parties.

This caused everyone to laugh, which enraged Ben, as he didn't like being the butt of any joke.

Anthony chimed in, "I love hearing about Ben's short comings, but Amanda and I are going to disappear for a while. And not a minute like Ben."

"Shut-up Anthony, you weren't even there," angrily yelled Ben.

"I guess neither were you," quipped Anthony.

Everyone exploded into laughter as Ben yelled back, "Fuck you man!"

"No thanks, I'll pass. I need a little more than a minute to take care of mine and my girls' needs," replied Anthony, which brought about even more laughter at Ben's expense, a situation that didn't usually happen, as some people were afraid of pissing him off due to his wealth and influence.

"Later ladies," stated Amanda as she smiled and walked with Anthony back to one of the spare bedrooms in the massive 10,000 square foot house on the lake.

The intimacy in their relationship had changed. Before, Anthony was concerned about taking care of Amanda's needs, but now, it was all about him. He wanted Amanda to take care of him multiple times and if she happened to be satisfied in the process, then she was lucky. Amanda wasn't happy about his new attitude and lack of respect, but she loved him and just hoped that in due time, the guy that she fell in love with would return.

Anthony and Amanda were gone for nearly 45 minutes before returning to join the rest of the guests at the party. As soon as Anthony was back, he began taking shots and chugging beers with anyone that would do so with him. And when everyone else refused to keep taking shots, Anthony didn't care as he continued by himself. Amanda tried to get Anthony to slow down, but he wouldn't listen. Now that he had gotten laid, all he cared about was getting as drunk as possible in order to forget about everything that was happening in his life.

Anthony had consumed an exorbitant amount of alcohol and was extremely intoxicated by the time he decided that he needed something to eat. And in his eyes, there was no better place at this time of the night than Gino's, which was an all-night sub shop that was owned and operated by an Italian family from New York. Their subs were delicious as they cut healthy portions of the meat in front of their patrons and used homemade bread fresh out of the oven. They had their own niche as they offered a variety of items that weren't available anywhere else in the area, especially their chicken finger sub which was made famous in Buffalo, NY. Gino's was a staple in Charlotte and an absolute favorite when someone was drunk and needed something to eat.

"Amanda, I'm hungry. Let's go to Gino's and get some food," insisted the inebriated Anthony.

Concerned, Amanda replied, "I don't think we should go anywhere, since both of us have been drinking. Neither of us is in any condition to drive."

"I'm fine to drive, so let's get my keys back from Brandon," stated Anthony as he slightly slurred his words.

"I don't think he'll give you your keys. You know how Ben is about people leaving his parties once they've started drinking."

"I don't care. If I want to leave, I'll do so. No one can tell me what to do," adamantly stated Anthony. Just then, he saw Brandon from across the room and yelled, "Brandon, where are my keys, I want to go get some food from Gino's."

Brandon knew that at some point someone usually asked for their keys, but as the sober voice of reason, he had to convince them that staying at the party was the best option. "That's not going to happen. You know I can't give anyone their keys back once they've been drinking."

"I don't give a fuck," yelled Anthony. "Either give me my keys or I'll have to take them from you or anyone else that tries to stop me. And everyone knows that nobody in here can beat me in a fight."

Brandon, who was no match physically for Anthony, was worried and tried to defuse the situation, "I don't want any trouble, but I still can't give you your keys."

After getting the wrong answer yet again, Anthony got up from his seat and began to walk towards Brandon, "Well, I guess we've got a problem and I'll have to kick your ass!"

Brandon quickly yelled for help, "Ben! Can you help me! Please convince Anthony that he's not going anywhere to get food tonight, at least not if he's driving."

Ben quickly made his way from across the room to try and diffuse the situation. "Anthony, I have tons of food. Go ahead and raid my fridge man. You don't need to go anywhere to eat."

Anthony exploded, "I don't care about the food anymore. I just want my keys!"

Ben tried to continue to calm Anthony down by talking some sense into him, "It's not going to happen tonight. You've had way too much to drink."

The three of them began arguing, which got everyone's attention. Nobody wanted to see a fight, as they knew that Anthony would win, which would probably result in the party coming to a screeching halt.

While the commotion was going on, Amanda snuck away to find Anthony's keys and make a phone call that might help prevent him from getting into serious trouble. Even though it was late, Amanda knew there was only one person who could help, Coach Tanzino. She dialed his number and waited for coach to pick up on the other end.

Vincent was sound asleep in bed as his cell phone began to ring, waking him up. Confused, he answered, "Hello."

"Coach T, it's Amanda, we need your help!"

Vincent quickly sat up, as the concern in her voice jolted him out of whatever remnants of sleep he'd just been in, causing adrenaline to rush through his veins, "What happened, what's going on?"

"Anthony's attempting to drive drunk and he's trying to fight everyone because they won't let him. Nobody's able to calm him down. You're the only one that can stop Anthony if he gets any worse. Can you please come and help us out?"

"Where are you at?"

"Ben's house," replied Amanda.

"I'll be over as fast as I can. Try to keep him as calm as possible and at Ben's house until I get there."

"Please hurry Coach. I don't know how much help I can be."

Vincent jumped out of bed and threw on the first pair of sweats he saw. He grabbed his keys and ran out the door. Vincent ignored all driving regulations because he knew that he only had a short period of time before Anthony would be uncontrollable by anyone but himself. As he arrived, he saw Anthony on the front lawn yelling and throwing anything that he could get his hands on. Vincent reacted quickly as he got out of his Jeep, leaving it in the middle of the road.

Once out of his Jeep, Vincent heard Anthony yelling, "This is my town, I own this place, no one can beat me."

Vincent quickly approached Anthony and yelled, "Anthony, what's going on?"

Anthony turned around to see Vincent rushing towards him. "What the fuck are you doing here Vincent? You want a piece of me too?"

"Why don't you get in the car with me?"

"No way, you'll have to beat me first."

"If that's what it takes," responded Vincent.

As Vincent reached him, Anthony took a swing. Vincent threw his arm by, making Anthony completely miss him. The force from the action caused Anthony to stumble and almost hit the ground.

Vincent didn't want to fight and tried to convince Anthony that it was a bad idea, "Come on Anthony, let's not do this."

"You're not my father. You don't have the right to tell me what to do!"

"I'm not trying to tell you what to do. I'm just trying to help."

"I don't need your help," adamantly yelled Anthony, as he was getting more upset with every waking moment.

Anthony took another swing at Vincent, but this time Vincent hit a duck under and ended up behind Anthony. Vincent immediately hit a suplex, sending Anthony flying through the air. As Anthony hit the ground, with Vincent on top, he began to squirm trying to regain control of his arms and get back to his feet, but he was unsuccessful as Vincent threw in both legs, a bar arm, and a half to prevent Anthony from being able to move at all. Anthony continued to kick and squirm, allowing Vincent's grip to tighten up, which was too much for Anthony to handle. After a minute of fighting, Anthony gave up.

Once he had been subdued, Vincent eased up his grip and let Anthony to his feet. Vincent held Anthony's arm behind his back as he walked him to his vehicle and put him in the back seat. Amanda joined Anthony in the back of coach's car as she tried to help keep Anthony calm. Anthony refused to speak; instead, he just sat there, upset and looking out the window as they distanced themselves from the party and all of the commotion that had been produced.

Vincent's first stop was Amanda's house to drop her off. As Amanda was exiting the vehicle, Vincent showed his appreciation for her help. "Amanda, thanks for calling me, please keep me informed of anything else. You can count on me to help out in any way that I can."

"Thanks Coach. I know he doesn't mean the things he says. I'm sorry that I had to wake you up."

"It's okay, I don't mind. I know he doesn't mean it. He's just going through some rough times. Just keep me posted if you ever need anything else."

"I will Coach. Anthony, I'll talk to you tomorrow. Call me, okay?"

But Anthony didn't respond. He just sat in the back seat sulking that Coach had embarrassed him in front of his friends and upset that Amanda was the reason why he arrived in the first place.

Vincent told Amanda goodbye and watched as she entered her house. Once she was safely inside, Coach began driving for home. Anthony didn't speak a word for the entire ride and Vincent was fine with it, as he wasn't up for another argument or to cause any further damage to their already strained relationship.

As they entered the house, Anthony immediately walked to his room, slammed the door and turned up his music. Knowing that he needed to get up in a short period of time for the tournament, Vincent decided to stay awake and prepare for the days matches.

However, as Vincent sat there, instead of concentrating on work, he couldn't help but think about Anthony and everything that he was going through. Vincent felt inadequate that he couldn't help ease Anthony's pain or find ways to help him. Unfortunately, Vincent felt as though Anthony believed that he was one of the problems instead of one of the solutions, which tugged at his heart, because it was the furthest from the truth. Vincent loved Anthony and only wanted to ease his pain and suffering by any means possible. Vincent knew that Anthony could have a long and happy life ahead of him, if he could just accept what had tragically happened and move beyond his grief.

Chapter Sixteen

Anthony's Demise

Thursday: December 11th, 2014

Anthony's decision to quit wrestling sent shockwaves across the halls of Parkside High School, throughout the state of North Carolina, and even to the collegiate ranks. Nobody felt this more than Anthony, who didn't like all of the added attention. He decided the solution to that problem was to skip his classes and basically ignore any rule that he felt was unnecessary to him anymore. He showed up when he felt like it and did as little or as much as he desired, which most of the time meant no work at all.

Rumors began to spread that his grades were rapidly dropping and were getting low enough in his required classes that his ability to graduate was in serious jeopardy, in-spite of having a 3.8 GPA entering his senior year. The once promising career of a young man was waiting in the balances. His life was spiraling out of control and, unfortunately, nobody was able to do anything about it.

Vincent was bothered by the entire situation, but he wasn't letting people know it. He kept a level head when he repeatedly had to answer questions on Anthony; his absences, his grades, and his overall lack of motivation to be a productive member of society. Anthony's relationship with Coach Tanzino had diminished under the new strains of their forced relationship, a relationship that Anthony wanted nothing to do with, while Vincent was doing whatever he possibly could to hold onto.

Anthony had a desire to be free from any and all parental support or presence; yet, he had to wait it out until his eighteenth birthday when he'd receive the rights to some of the money left to him by his parents. Until then, he was going to defy whomever he wanted and do exactly as he pleased, no matter who he hurt in the process. Vincent took the brunt of this as he had lost the friends who he considered family in Terrance and Olivia and now in jeopardy of losing the friendship that he had with their son Anthony. A young man that Vincent had grown to love and treat as if he was his own flesh and blood; who he gave everything he had to provide him with the ability to further his talents at the next level and was on track to earn a scholarship to any university of his choice, before that fateful night ripped all of it away, shattering the hopes and dreams that he had worked so hard at achieving.

Vincent had little to no control over what Anthony was doing, even though he was living under his roof. This tore Vincent apart, realizing that this once promising student-athlete was heading down a very dark and dangerous path. A path that Vincent had no way of stopping, in-spite of him living in the same house.

As Anthony's guardian, Vincent was taking flak from the school's administration and some of the other teachers, for his lack of control of Anthony. They questioned Vincent repeatedly as to what he was doing to provide a safe and healthy environment for Anthony to cope with his issues. All of which continued to add more stress and pressure on Vincent, but he tried to hide the pain that he was feeling along with the problems that this entire situation had thrust upon him. Vincent was truly doing everything in his power to keep it all together for Anthony as he was hopeful that Anthony would soon recover from all of this and pick up the pieces of his life, ultimately righting the ship that he was in danger of capsizing or even sinking into an abyss.

Anthony wasn't turning in any work, refused to study for tests and began becoming a disturbance in all of his classes. He was even being sent to In School Suspension for his behavior. He was being kept at school instead of being placed on Out of School Suspension because of Vincent and his plea to the administration to understand what the young man was going through. Vincent did everything he could to convince everyone that he was still the same kid that everyone had grown to know and love as he also continued to reassure everyone that he was helping Anthony deal with all of his issues and that soon enough they'd see a difference in him. However, they were just words because most of the time Vincent didn't even believe what he was trying to sell.

All Vincent could do was hold onto the hope that God hadn't done all of this to destroy Anthony, but to make him a better man. He prayed and hoped that it wouldn't take too long for Anthony to realize that he could take this negative situation and turn it into a positive, or for Anthony's true character and fate to come to fruition; therefore, preventing irreprehensible consequences from diminishing Anthony's bright future.

Chapter Seventeen

Anthony's Scholarship

Thursday: December 18, 2014

Vincent had just arrived home from a hard practice when his phone rang. On the other end was Don Simpson, one of Vincent's former college teammates, who had become one of their alma mater's highly regarded assistant coaches and recruiters ever since his collegiate career had ended. Vincent and Don had spoken many times on the possibility of Anthony wrestling at WVU. However, many of the other programs were losing interest in Anthony due to his absence from the sport, but Don hadn't lost his desire and wanted to see where everything stood with this extremely talented student-athlete.

They became good friends when Vincent was on his recruiting trip to WVU, as Don was his host, and their friendship had grown significantly over the years. Don worked hard at finding talented wrestlers throughout the country and relied heavily on WVU's alumni, especially the former wrestlers, who wanted nothing more than to help build the program into a national powerhouse.

As Vincent answered his phone, he heard a familiar and chipper voice on the other end. "Hey Vincent, how are things going?"

"Things are alright," replied Vincent, as he tried to hide the problems that he was actually dealing with.

"I've been hearing rumors that Anthony quit. Is that true? Is he planning on continuing his wrestling career?" wondered Don.

"With everything that's gone on with his parents, I don't think he'll be wrestling in the near future, he needs to work out the fact that his parents are gone. It's a lot for a kid to handle."

"I can understand that. But it disappoints me and a lot of other people. You know as well as I do that he has the ability to be a college All-American, if not more."

"I know. We've worked so hard over the past few years to groom him for the next level. He's already an even better wrestler than I ever was. Anthony's way ahead of the curve when it comes to his ability to adapt to all situations on the mat. He's able to learn moves instantly and he perfects them in no time at all."

"Vincent, you don't have to sell me on him. I know all of this and so does every other college coach out there, but the real question is, will he return to the mat?"

Vincent wondered the same thing ever since Anthony quit, but as the days turned into weeks, Vincent's hopes of Anthony's return were dwindling. But for Anthony's benefit, he didn't want colleges to lose interest, in the off chance that he decided to return. "I believe he will when the time is right. He just needs to cope with the grieving process. Please don't give up on him. It'll be worth your while in the long run," assured Vincent.

"For you, I'll keep things open on our end and let the coaches know that he's just taking a short time off to grieve the loss of his parents, but he intends to return and finish out the season. But, that will only last for a little while. I hope you're right and he returns before his season's completely lost."

"I know. I'm sorry to put you in this predicament. I just hope people can understand that this is a tough time for him. He needs to mourn the loss of his parents now, so that it doesn't affect him later in life. I promise that he'll be back in time for the end of the season and to have that rematch with Jamie Wright," stated Vincent.

This seemed to work, as Don was willing to keep the lines of communication open and continue to have Anthony on the top of their list of recruits. It was a gamble, but one that could pay huge dividends in the long run.

They spoke for a few more minutes about Anthony and the rest of the Parkside Mustangs, as Don had his eyes on a few other members of the team. He was looking towards the future and felt as though anyone that Vincent coached would have a distinct advantage over other prospective college wrestlers. This was why Don was hoping that their friendship could produce a successful pipeline of talent from North Carolina to West Virginia University.

As Vincent ended the phone call and set his phone down, he couldn't help but think about their conversation. Even though Vincent had continuously reassured Don that Anthony would return, unfortunately, he had serious doubts that it would actually occur. Vincent knew that it was an atrocity, as Anthony was well on his way of becoming one of the greatest wrestlers to ever compete in the sport and primed to achieve an unbelievable amount of success at the collegiate and the international levels.

Chapter Eighteen

The Parkside Invitational Tournament (All-Star Classic)

Saturday: December 20th, 2014

On Saturday December 20th, sixteen teams arrived at Parkside High School for the Parkside Invitational Tournament. The tournament was a who's who of the top teams and wrestlers representing five different states. Many people had nicknamed it "The All-Star Classic" as the best of the best in the states of North Carolina, South Carolina, Virginia, Georgia and West Virginia were participating in the tournament. A number of college recruiters were in attendance to watch many of the top notch athletes' battle each other throughout the day.

The Parkside Invitational hosted five of the top thirty recruits in the nation. Three of which were still uncommitted to what college they'd continue their careers at. Had Anthony been there, he'd have made it six of the top thirty recruits and the highest ranked recruit of them all as he was widely considered one of the best wrestlers, if not the best in the nation.

The tournament presented quite a challenge as even first round matches pitted state qualifiers against each other. In total, the tournament boasted fifteen athletes that had a combined twenty state championships, thirty more wrestlers who were at least a one-time state place winner and an additional twenty state qualifiers, making it even tougher than most individual state championship tournaments. These coaches weren't afraid to have their wrestlers take a loss; instead, they felt that this was a good test of their skills and what improvements or adjustments needed to be made at the midway point of the season, prior to the final push to their respective state tournaments.

Vincent did a great job of inviting the best competition for his tournament. He felt as though if he was going to spend the time hosting an event, that he'd make it worth his while. A few of the teams that came from out of town had connections to West Virginia University as one of the coaches, or a parent of one of the wrestlers, had gone to college there. This made it easier to bring in these elite programs and convince them that the drive to Charlotte, North Carolina would be worth their while.

These were also teams and coaches that Vincent had gotten to know throughout the off-season as some of them hosted tournaments that Vincent brought the Mustang Wrestling Club to. They figured it was only fair to travel to each other's tournaments; besides, the coaches knew that these events were great experiences for their athletes.

The tournament was supposed to include a rematch of the State Championship finals match between Jamie Wright and Anthony Williams as Jamie's team, the Pinehurst Panthers, were invited by Coach Tanzino on Anthony's request during the off-season. Anthony wanted his chance to beat Jamie in front of his home crowd before he did so again at the state championships. However, it was a match that wouldn't be seen on this day, if ever again.

As the tournament progressed, it was evident that most of the North Carolina teams weren't fairing that well against the highly regarded competition from the out-of-state. Even though there were more North Carolina teams in the field of sixteen, Georgia and Virginia were clearly taking over the tournament, with the exception of Vincent's Mustangs.

The Mustangs were the only North Carolina team that had any overall success. Besides them, the lone wrestler from North Carolina that did extremely well was Jamie Wright, who was completely dominating the competition in what was clearly the toughest weight class of the tournament. The 160 pound weight class boasted four state champions and six others who were place winners from their respective state. This included Quinton Smith of the Fulton Thrashers, who was nationally ranked, and Mark Anderson from Myrtle Beach, who was also a highly sought after college prospect. Both of them had been easily beaten by Anthony Williams throughout the off-season and now had suffered the same fate at the hands of Jamie Wright. Mark lost a 12-3 major decision loss to Jamie in the semi-finals, while Quinton was beaten 11-5 in the finals. However, neither match was as close as the scores appeared.

Even though the 160 pound weight class was laden with talent, it was still expected that Jamie Wright and Anthony Williams would've met in the finals. Unfortunately for the crowd and the scouts, it wasn't meant to be.

Instead, Jamie felt satisfaction when he beat Dante Adams, Anthony's former backup, in the quarterfinals of the tournament. But the match wasn't as one sided as many would have expected as Dante gave Jamie a run for his money for most of the match. It wasn't until the end of the third period that Jamie hit a five point move to gain a major decision. This convinced Vincent that had Anthony been there, he would've easily beaten Jamie.

Yet, Jamie was up to the challenge as he demolished his highly touted opponents. His success led him directly down the path to a tournament championship and also brandished him with the Most Outstanding Wrestler Award. His dominance impressed a number of scouts in the stands who were there to see Anthony and Jamie clash. Instead, Jamie stole the show and earned himself some respect in his goal of achieving a repeat state championship and a college scholarship.

Besides Jamie Wright, Parkside was the only other team in North Carolina to have an individual champion as they had three: Chris States at 120, Tim Ridley at 170, and Ryan Thompson at Heavyweight, along with two runners-up: Matt States at 106 and Mike Robinson at 220.

Georgia was able to match North Carolina with four champions, three of which came from the Fulton Thrashers in the 152, 195 and 220 weight classes, while the 138 pound champion was from the Savannah Snakes. Virginia had three champions; two coming from the Richmond Raptors, at 126 and 132 pounds, who also ended with a third place finish as a team. While another champion at 182 pounds was added from the Virginia Beach Rattlers.

South Carolina earned two champions of their own, one from Myrtle Beach at 106 pounds and the other from Charleston at 145 pounds. While West Virginia was able to earn a lone tournament champion at 113 pounds, who hailed from University High School out of Morgantown. Even though eight of the sixteen teams were from North Carolina, Parkside was the only one from the area to finish in the top five, showing the dominance of the out of state competition.

The team race had remained tight throughout the entire competition, but the Parkside Mustangs were able to pull off a first place finish by the slimmest of margins, a half point, over the Fulton Thrashers who were from Atlanta, Georgia. Even though both teams had three champions, the difference came from bonus point victories, a statistic that Vincent was extremely proud of as he prided his athletes in their desire to strive for more and their ability to press the action all the way to the final whistle.

This first place finish, at such an elite tournament, was a huge step in Vincent being recognized as one of the best high school coaches. Vincent enjoyed the praise, but felt that his recognition benefitted his athletes as he used the exposure as another means to get them recruited, as college coaches were regularly following their progress.

Vincent's name was even being thrown around to take over various college programs. But at this point in time, Vincent wasn't concerned with that. He enjoyed being in Charlotte and at Parkside High School. He felt as though he was making a bigger difference with his students and athletes than he could do if he took over a college program. But it wasn't completely out of the realm of possibilities that in the future he'd consider the move to the collegiate ranks.

The Mustangs barely won the tournament, but had Anthony been there, he'd have surely helped open the gap between them and the rest of the competition. In-spite of Anthony's absence, Vincent felt good about the results. His team was coming up big as they were grinding out victories against every challenge they were presented. Vincent even felt positive about some of the losses as his athletes never gave up and fought with everything they had. Many of them had pulled off upsets or even gave a state champion or a place winner a run for his money throughout the tournament. Both of which, Vincent felt were building blocks that would catapult his team to being considered an elite program.

At the end of the tournament, as the Mustangs were breaking down the mats and cleaning up the gym, Jamie Wright approached Coach Tanzino. His message was short and sweet as he called Anthony a chicken for not wrestling. Jamie's confidence and arrogance was in full display as he believed that Anthony shouldn't even return as he didn't have a prayer in the world of taking the 160 pound state championship away from him. The smug look on his face irritated Vincent, but he didn't let him know it.

Vincent knew not to stoop to the level of an insolent teenager who didn't understand how to respect his elders; instead, he just smiled at Jamie as he spewed such boisterous words. Vincent remained silent, letting the cocky high schooler think he was invincible. Jamie's coach noticed what was going on and didn't like what he saw. He liked Jamie's fire and arrogance, but it wasn't acceptable for him to talk to another coach that way, especially one who was Vincent's caliber. He quickly approached them to defuse the situation and apologize to Vincent for his athletes disrespect.

As Jamie was escorted away by his coach, he held on tight to the large MOW trophy. Vincent couldn't help but hope that Anthony returned to prove Jamie wrong because he knew that Anthony was the best high school wrestler that he'd ever seen. But he wasn't alone as most college coaches also agreed with his sentiment, which was why Anthony was considered a much bigger prospect than Jamie Wright.

Vincent was pleased with the day, as he had seen many promising aspects of his team. Their grit and determination had made Vincent proud to be there coach. But deep down inside, a nagging feeling was trying to thwart his happiness as he couldn't take his mind off of Anthony. Vincent had been doing his best to keep this hidden from everyone, but he was worried that he wouldn't be able to keep up the front much longer. All he could hope was that Anthony would return before things got any worse, as Vincent wanting nothing more than to see Anthony back on the mat pursuing his dreams. Anthony had worked so hard at achieving them, that he hated seeing all of his talent thrown in the gutter. Besides, Vincent knew that Anthony would indubitably regret it for the rest of his life if he didn't return in time to finish out his senior season.

Chapter Nineteen

The Spiral Continues

Tuesday: December 23rd, 2014

As darkness drew upon the Parkside community, another party was in the works. Anthony and Ben had a Christmas party planned for the evening as they knew that the first night of their vacation was the perfect opportunity to celebrate. The usual crew was going to be arriving shortly, which urged Ben and Anthony to make the final preparations that included purchasing the alcohol. Ben had always been able to buy alcohol at a local liquor store, because they barely checked identification from its patrons. However, even if they did check, Ben had stolen his cousin's driver's license, which always worked for him as they resembled one another.

As Anthony and Ben finished setting up for the party, Ben asked, "You going to drive me to get the booze?"

"Yeah, not a problem," replied Anthony, as he couldn't wait to have an alcoholic beverage in his hand and would do whatever was needed to get it.

"Alright, let's head out now. Everyone should be arriving in about an hour."

"What about the watermelon and the vodka?" questioned Anthony, as he was referring to the watermelon that they had cut a hole in and placed a bottle of vodka upside down in, letting the vodka soak into the fruit. It allowed every bite of the watermelon to ooze with vodka and a quick way to get people intoxicated.

Ben thought about it for a moment before replying, "Let it soak a little bit longer. That'll make it extremely potent."

"Everyone's going to love the fruit that fucks you up," replied Anthony, with a smile on his face, as he knew he would be.

"Of course! It's only going to help make Ben's Christmas Bonanza legendary!" exclaimed Ben, who was a master of throwing parties.

"I know I will," proclaimed Anthony as he began to head towards the door, "let's hurry up and get some alcohol so we can kick things off. You have enough money?"

Ben didn't even have to check his pockets as he knew that he had plenty of cash. As they walked out of the house, Ben smugly replied, "Yeah, of course I do. I made a few hundred dollars off of the last party. Besides, my parents are gone again and they left me food money. I mean, who spends $200 in a couple of days on food. Man they're dumb sometimes."

They both laughed as they got into Anthony's car. Anthony drove Ben the four miles to the liquor store, where he bought eight cases of beer, three bottles of wine, and two bottles of flavored Vodka, along with Rum, Tequila, and a few mixers to go along with the alcohol. Once again, Ben had no problems buying the drinks, because the old man who ran the store was working. He had seen Ben so often that he didn't even look at his license anymore. As Ben walked out with his cart full of alcohol, Anthony got out of his car to help load all of the booze into the trunk. They both knew that the evening was guaranteed to be full of excitement as everyone was bound to be extremely intoxicated.

By the time Ben and Anthony arrived back at Ben's house, they saw that some of the guests were already waiting for the hosts to show up with the beverages. They weren't even out of the car when they heard Josh yell, "Dudes, what took you so long? We want to get our drink on!"

"We're here now, that's all that matters," replied Ben, who proceeded to open up the trunk, "and here's the alcohol. Now help me carry it into the house."

Josh and a couple of the other guys quickly went over to Anthony's car, each grabbing something to carry.

As Brittany noticed what Ben had purchased, she exclaimed, "Yummy, looks like you got my favorite, Rum and Coke!"

Jackie was also excited, "Yeah, me too, Vodka-Cranberry, nicely done Ben."

Ben smiled, "Anything to please the ladies."

"What a ladies man," laughed Jackie.

"Or so he thinks," laughed Brittany, as she walked over to Ben and gave him a big hug and a kiss.

"I'm glad that everyone's happy to see each other, but times wasting, let's drink," interjected Josh as he had a case of beer in each hand and made his way towards Ben's front door.

Ben quickly responded, "Hold your horses, let me get my money and then you guys can drink the night away."

Josh handed Ben a ten dollar bill, as was the customary going rate for a guy to drink at one of Ben's parties. The rest followed suit, handing money over to Ben before cracking open their first beverage. Amanda had come with Brandon, while Anthony helped Ben get things set up. Anthony thanked Brandon for bringing his girlfriend to the party as he walked up to Amanda, giving her a big hug and a kiss, while letting his hands wander down to her butt.

Anthony and Amanda remained outside for a few minutes to talk and spend a little time alone, while everyone else went inside to begin drinking and playing games.

"So babe, did you miss me?" asked Anthony.

"Of course I did," replied Amanda as she was sad that Anthony had skipped another day of school. "I wish you made it to school today. Then I would've been able to spend more time with you."

"I'm tired of that scene. Everyone's either, 'ah poor baby' or yelling at me for wasting my life."

"Everyone's just concerned, because they want the old Anthony back."

"He's gone and so are his parents. Listen, I don't want to talk about this. I'm here to have fun, so let's do that."

All Amanda could say was, "Okay," as she felt dejected from the lack of respect Anthony now showed everyone and his inability to communicate with her anymore. As they entered the house, the music was blasting as the party was already in full swing. People were dancing, making out, and playing cards. As Anthony and Amanda sat down to join the intense game of asshole, Anthony immediately won the first hand, giving him the presidency and control of the other players. He took his position of power seriously as he made sure to make as many people drink and get annihilated as rapidly as possible.

He called out for everyone to drink almost every time that their alcoholic beverage had been removed from their lip, which made for more drinking than actual playing of the game.

"Hey asshole, drink for skipping the president," demanded Anthony, as Aisha had played a ten to match the previous card on the pile, causing Anthony to be skipped and forcing him to take a drink of his beer.

She did as was commanded of her by Anthony, before asking, "Are you trying to get me drunk?"

Anthony laughed, "Isn't that the object of the game?"

"Yeah," answered Aisha, with a smile on her face.

"Then stop complaining and drink again for talking back," ordered Anthony.

No sooner had Aisha removed the beer bottle from her lips when Josh called out, "Nice, a four has been laid down. It's waterfall time!"

The group playing the game immediately began participating in a waterfall, in which everyone keeps drinking until the person prior to them stops, allowing the next person in line to stop when they chose to, and so on down the line. They went in a clockwise order, just like the order they were following to play the game. Ultimately, this caused the individual at the end of the line to drink most, if not all, of their beverage, and rapidly increased how intoxicated everyone got.

As the game continued, so did Anthony's intensity and abuse of the others. Unfortunately for them, he kept winning, causing him to remain as the president and in complete control of the situation. "Beer Bitch, I'm out of beer, grab me one, and grab one for everyone else," demanded Anthony.

"Alright man. Why haven't we gotten the cooler out, so that I don't have to keep getting up every few minutes?" asked Josh as he got up to get more alcohol.

Bothered by the statement, Anthony yelled, "Stop complaining and just get the booze!"

Josh quickly made his way to the fridge, which housed all of the alcohol, and grabbed enough beers for everyone to have one and a few people to have a second. As he returned, he handed everyone a cold beverage. But for Anthony, it wasn't done in a timely manner, which upset him. "Nice job bitch, now drink for taking so long to get me my beer," commanded Anthony.

Josh did as he was instructed, which he didn't mind, as he wanted nothing more than to get wasted.

The group continued to play asshole until Anthony came up with the idea to switch to something that could become a bit more entertaining, Truth or Dare. He'd been making people drink excessive amounts of alcohol, so why not make them do even more. Everyone agreed that a change was in order, as they had been constantly abused for the past hour by Anthony while he was the president. They thought that Truth or Dare was the best option, because they believed that Anthony couldn't take complete control of the situation any longer, or at least they hoped that he couldn't.

They moved to Ben's living room, which was separate from where the rest of the patrons were partying. This gave them a little more privacy to do as they pleased. As the game of Truth or Dare continued, the type of questions and dares became more intimate and extremely sexual. Everyone sat and enjoyed the show as they watched Jackie give Brandon a lap dance, prior to Brittany having to flash the group. Josh was given the task of running around Ben's house naked while everyone laughed and cheered him on.

At first Amanda wasn't bothered with the game as she was continuously answering questions instead of taking a dare; however, Anthony was more interested in the dares. As the intensity grew, so did Amanda's problem with the game. Anthony's turn came up, and he once again chose dare, instead of the truth, but this time, Amanda didn't like what she heard, as Anthony was dared to kiss Aisha by Josh. Initially Amanda didn't react, seeing how Anthony would handle the situation, but when Anthony and Aisha began to make-out instead of just kiss, she got extremely pissed and stormed off.

Anthony was enjoying his kiss with Aisha too much to even care that Amanda had left, especially since he'd been flirting with Aisha all night long. The game continued on as everyone ignored the fact that Amanda had disappeared, but before too long, the group began to lose steam as there weren't enough new ideas for dares that any of them could come up with. This convinced Anthony to find Amanda and see what was bothering her.

Anthony looked around the enormous residence, and eventually discovered Amanda in one of the spare rooms. Anthony tried to defend his actions as it was only a game, but Amanda wanted nothing to do with his excuses. She made sure he realized how much he'd changed over the past month, and was hurting her feelings as she unconditionally loved him and didn't feel as though he was treating her right anymore. But Anthony didn't want to hear any of this, as he stormed out of the room. He didn't want to listen to another speech on how he should go back to being like he was, because life wasn't like it was a month ago. Everything was different now and unfortunately for him, it could never be as it once was.

After their fight, Anthony decided to get obliterated, because it seemed like the best way for him to forget about all of his problems. He started chugging beers, eating the watermelon, and taking shots of whatever was nearby. After an hour of throwing back as much alcohol as he could consume, Anthony began to feel sick.

He quickly ran to Ben's bathroom and started to throw up all over the place. Even though he was aiming for the toilet, most of the vomit managed to make its way onto the floor and all over his clothes. Anthony remained on the floor, barely moving at all, for almost 30 minutes before Brittany discovered him. She immediately grabbed Amanda and showed her where Anthony was and the condition he was in.

Amanda was upset at what he had done to himself, and how he had treated her, but in-spite of it all, she loved him. She tried to help out by attempted to clean him up, but was unsuccessful. "Anthony, we need to get you home," stated Amanda.

Anthony was agitated and he didn't want anything to do with her or anyone else. "Leave me alone, what do you care, what does anyone care?" stated Anthony as he slurred his words.

"I'm not going to sit here and listen to you abuse me. I'm leaving, you can take care of yourself for once!" exclaimed Amanda as she ran out of the bathroom crying. She was upset at how much Anthony had changed. He was constantly treating her poorly and he completely ignored how much she loved and cared for him. Amanda was one of the only people that truly had his best interests in mind, but instead of him opening up to her in his time of need she took the brunt of his anger.

Amanda left Anthony in the bathroom, still covered in his own filth and vomit. He didn't even notice that she'd left him to manage the situation on his own. He just remained there, looking pathetic and hopeless. After she walked out of the bathroom, Amanda grabbed her cell phone to dial Coach Tanzino's number, because he was the only one with the patience or ability to cope with Anthony anymore.

Vincent's cell phone began ringing, once again waking him up in the middle of the night. As he grabbed the phone, he noticed that it was Amanda calling him. Realizing that Anthony wasn't home, he knew there was a problem. "What's wrong?" asked Vincent immediately.

"Anthony and I are fighting and he's being an asshole to everyone tonight. He's currently throwing up all over Ben's bathroom and is telling everyone off. I'm sorry to call you so late again, but I don't know who else to turn to."

"It's okay, that's what I'm here for. Do I need to come get him?" asked Vincent.

"You might need to, because everyone's pretty mad at him right now."

"Alright, I'm on my way," stating Vincent as he pulled the covers off of him.

"Thanks Coach, I won't be here when you arrive, so please take care of him."

"I will Amanda."

"Coach, you're the best, he doesn't deserve you for everything you're doing for him," stated Amanda, as she knew that Coach was being treated even worse than she was.

"I know he's going through a tough time. I'm just going to have to help him get through it, no matter how long it takes. Besides, I love him."

"Thanks again. I'll give you a call tomorrow to find out how Anthony's doing."

"Okay, I'll talk to you then and thanks for helping Anthony. He might not be himself right now, but I know he loves you," reassured Vincent, as he knew how hard this was on her and how poorly Anthony had been treating her, which she didn't deserve as she had done so much for him as well as being such a sweet person.

"Thanks Coach, I know he does." And with that Amanda ended the call.

Vincent immediately got out of bed and found some clothes to throw on. He didn't even attempt to wake up Vanessa and tell her the details, as she remained sound asleep on the other side of the bed. He just quickly got ready and walked out of his house, jumped into his Jeep, and sped off towards Ben's place.

When he arrived, he was greeted by a group of intoxicated Parkside High School students calling out "Coach," which was echoed repeatedly by the guests as he walked through the house. This wasn't an ideal situation for a teacher and a coach to be walking through a house full of underage students and athletes drinking or doing even worse. But he had no other choice under the current circumstances. His immediate desire was to find Anthony and get him home. Vincent simply asked, "Where's Anthony?" as he inquired into his whereabouts.

Josh was the first to respond, "In Ben's bathroom, straight down that hallway. You come to get him?"

"Yeah, I'll take care of him," replied Vincent as he headed in the directions that Josh had pointed him in.

As Vincent entered the bathroom, he saw Anthony hugging the toilet. His shirt and pants were completely covered in vomit, snot, and sweat. He didn't even open his eyes or react to someone coming into the restroom. It was a grim sight as he just hoped that Anthony didn't need to be brought to the hospital to have his stomach pumped.

"Anthony, how are you feeling?" asked Vincent.

Anthony wasn't able to make out the figure, but he recognized the voice. He barely moved as he rudely replied, "Who the hell called you? I don't need you around!"

"Don't worry about who called me, just know I'm here. Your friends care about you. They're concerned and want you taken care of."

Anthony was agitated that Vincent was there. He just wanted to be left alone. He took a guess at who could've called him, "Amanda called you, didn't she?"

"It doesn't matter who called, let's just get you cleaned up and back home."

Anthony refused, "No way, I'm not going to your place."

"You don't have a choice, because you can't spend the night in Ben's bathroom."

"What do you care?" angrily responded Anthony.

Hating that he even had to respond to such a question, "I'm just trying to help out. That's why you were left in my care by your parents."

This struck Anthony to the core, "My parents should still be alive! It's not fair!"

Vincent knew he was right, but there wasn't anything that could be done to change the situation. "No it's not, but we must do the best with the hand that's dealt to us by God."

This upset Anthony even more than he already was, "God, why would he take my parents from me? I still need them!"

"God didn't do it to be mean, it was just their time. I think he wanted to challenge you, to see how you'd handle yourself in tough times."

The last thing that Anthony wanted to hear was some kind of lecture or Vincent rationalizing the situation. "Screw that, and screw you. You're not my father, your nothing to me anymore. I've just been forced to stay at your shithole that you call a house until I can get my money and move out on my own."

Vincent shrugged off his comments, as he knew that Anthony was drunk and upset. "I know you really don't mean that, you just miss your parents, which is normal."

"Why'd they have to die?" questioned Anthony as tears streamed down his face.

"People die, but what you do in remembrance keeps them alive in your heart and your mind. I'm not here to be your father, just your friend. How about we make our way back to my shithole and get you washed up before we try to sober you up."

Vincent knelt down to pick Anthony up off of the floor. Once up, he led him out of Ben's house and into his Jeep. As they traveled back to Coach's place, Anthony left his head outside the window as he profusely threw up anything that had previously remained in his stomach.

After arriving home, he got Anthony upstairs and into the shower, where he helped wash him up before assisting him to throw on a fresh pair of clothes. Vincent placed Anthony in bed with some towels and a trash can next to him just in case Anthony needed to be sick in the middle of the night. He sat and observed the incoherent Anthony for a while as he slept. Vincent wanted to make sure that Anthony was going to be alright before leaving the room.

After sitting there for nearly an hour, Vincent finally got back into his bed to get some sleep, but sat up for most of the night thinking of ways in which he could help Anthony get back on the right path. This was completely wearing on Vincent, as it was taking an exorbitant amount of energy to take care of someone he loves, but wanted nothing to do with him.

Questions swirled in Vincent's head at a dizzying pace and no answers seemed to be in sight. It was truly the most trying time in Anthony's life, but it was also that way for Vincent. He hadn't expected to be responsible for a teenager who was going through so much. But Vincent knew that God wouldn't place more on his plate than he could handle. He just needed to find the strength to continue on for as long as Anthony needed to get through the grieving process, which unfortunately didn't appear to be coming to an end anytime soon.

Chapter Twenty

New Year's Eve

Wednesday: December 31, 2014

Nothing had changed in the week and a half since Anthony's debacle at the Christmas party. Anthony was still doing whatever he wanted, which angered most of his friends because of how he was treating them, but they figured this was the way someone grieved the loss of their parents. Even though he was treating everyone with an utmost disregard, nobody considered standing up to him or telling him otherwise. Most of them seemed to walk on eggshells around him, letting Anthony do as he pleased. They just continued to enable him to act with a complete lack of disregard for others. He'd turned into someone that was unrecognizable by those who had known him for years.

New Year's is thought of as a time for people to think about the possibilities of new beginnings as they gain a fresh start in a New Year. Nobody could use that fresh start more than Anthony, but it was the furthest from his mind. All he could think about was the New Year's Eve party that was taking place at Brittany's house.

Ben's parents were extremely upset after the last party, forcing Ben to take a break from hosting another one. However, Brittany's parents were fine with hosting. Her house was a two story 2,100 square foot home, with a basement. The basement was set up as a game room, which consisted of a pool table, couches, and a big screen television. There was also a spare bedroom and a bar, which was always fully stocked by Brittany's parents, mainly because they regularly hosted social gatherings of their own.

Otherwise, the basement was primarily used by Brittany and her friends. Her parents were laid back when it came to her and her friends drinking at the house. They sometimes even got permission from the other kids' parents to allow them to drink and spend the night there. But tonight was a little different, as it had been a last minute change in venues. However, that didn't keep any of the usual crew from being in attendance.

Anthony showed up with Amanda and brought his dog Sammie along for the night, which didn't bother anyone as they loved the boxer. The party wasn't outrageous like the normal gatherings, which for the most part seemed to be fine with everyone for once. They all spent time drinking, playing pool, and watching the New Year's festivities in Times Square. But as the night progressed, everyone started to get a little drunk, and a bit bored. Everyone began throwing out a variety of ideas for games they could play to liven up the festivities.

Nobody could agree on what to do until Josh spoke up. "Hey everyone, I've got an idea, let's go steel some lawn ornaments! We can split up into two teams and see which one gets the best and the most lawn ornaments."

Ben immediately loved the idea as he jumped up off of the couch, "I love it! What are the teams?"

"Me, Aisha, Brandon, and Jackie versus Ben, Sam, and Brittany," stated Josh.

"What about Anthony and Amanda?" asked Ben.

Anthony replied, "I'm not in guys, Sammie just went outside and I'm going to grab him. Amanda, if you want to go, you can."

Amanda was excited to hear that Anthony was okay with her joining everyone else, "I'll go with Brittany."

Happy that Amanda would join them, Brittany began to talk trash to the others, "Great, because we're going to kick your asses!"

Everyone laughed as they started to go back and forth about which team would win and how to determine the winner. Everyone seemed to be fine with Anthony not joining, as he had been nothing but trouble as of late.

But, before they left, Ben checked to make sure that Anthony didn't miss out on anything. "Are you sure you don't want to join in?" questioned Ben.

"Yeah, I'll be alright here. I'll see you guys when you get back," replied Anthony. As he almost felt that some alone time would be good for him.

This was a little out of the ordinary for the way that Anthony had been acting lately, which caused Amanda to worry. "Are you sure you're okay?" she wondered.

Without hesitation, but with a solemn tone, Anthony replied, "Yeah, I'll be fine. Go have fun." Even though she wasn't completely satisfied with his answer, she took it. At least he wasn't being mean or yelling at her for caring. Amanda proceeded to hug and kiss Anthony as she told him that she loved him and he told her the same in return.

As everyone went upstairs to their cars, Anthony walked out of the basement door, which led to a set of stairs and into the backyard. As Anthony reached the backyard, he felt the brisk evening air hit his face as he called out for Sammie, but he didn't see or hear anything. Anthony continued to walk around the house, searching for his companion, until he reached the path which led through the woods behind Brittany's house. He took a swig from the bottle of Vodka that he was carrying with him, to warm him up from the chill in the air, before once again calling out to Sammie. This time, he heard a bark coming from somewhere in the distance. Anthony instinctively started traveling through the darkness of the woods to find Sammie, wherever he was.

The further he traveled through the woods, the louder the barking got from Sammie, but no matter how many times Anthony called out his name, he wouldn't come back to him. Anthony had never really gone this far into the woods before, so he was unsure where it led to. But he needed to get Sammie, as he was the lone remnants of a life that he once had.

As he progressed, Anthony noticed an opening in the path, which appeared to be some type of a field. As he made it past the clearing, he could see that Sammie had gone through a fence, and was sitting down looking at something. But Anthony couldn't make it out, as it was too dark and somewhat foggy that evening.

Anthony called out, "Sammie, come on boy, come here," but there was no luck, as Sammie didn't move. Anthony was clearly aggravated with the situation, as he spoke to himself, "Fine, I'll come get you."

Anthony crept underneath the fence, not realizing where he was going, except that he wanted to grab the last remaining memento from his parents. As Anthony approached Sammie, he realized where he was, the Parkside Cemetery. Anthony hadn't been back since the funeral, because he refused to be reminded of their tragedy. As he stood next to Sammie, he looked at what his dog was facing; it was his parent's cemetery plot and their headstone.

Anthony took a long hard look at it before reading the eternal words that were etched on their headstone. "In loving memory of the greatest parents anyone could have. They were kind, generous, and loving people who welcomed everyone into their lives and their hearts."

Anthony dropped the bottle of Vodka that he'd been carrying with him as he fell to his knees, instantly beginning to cry. He broke down into a never-ending river of tears, as the emotions of the past month and a half rushed over him, emotions that he'd been harvesting and preventing from reaching the surface since the day of their accident.

Anthony sat there crying and staring at the grave, sitting on top of the land that entombed his parents. As Anthony continued to cry, Sammie cuddled up next to him, as he knew how sad his owner was. Anthony remained on the ground, as memories flashed before his eyes. He remembered the good times that they had while he was growing up, the looks on his parents faces each and every match no matter the outcome, their positive feedback and attitude, and all of the sacrifices they made to provide the best possible life for him.

He realized that his parents had placed him in the custody of Coach Tanzino because he was family to them and the only person that they trusted to look out for his best interest. He thought about the times that Coach gave up his own plans to help him or provide him with an opportunity to succeed. Anthony realized that Vincent had put his life on hold for him on numerous occasions and most importantly had taken him in after the loss of his parents. But all he'd done repeatedly was cause more problems and hurt the man that was the only family that he had left, even though Vincent was just trying to do what he could to make the best of the situation, while providing a roof over his head and an environment conducive to him healing from all of the pain.

After a while, Anthony cried himself to sleep as he remained next to the headstone and on top of the grave where his parents were buried. Sammie never left his side; instead, he curled his body against Anthony's, providing warmth for the two of them.

After two hours of their adventure, everyone returned to Brittany's house. They had stolen a ton of lawn ornaments and decided to place them all on the front lawn of the Williams' former house as a way to honor Anthony. They took pictures with their cellphones so that they could show him when they returned. They set up a farm scene, a Chinese village, Snow White and the Seven Dwarfs, even a fire hydrant made its way to the front yard. All of which made for a significant amount of stolen property that could have gotten all of them into some serious trouble. But they didn't think about that, they were just being reckless teenagers. Besides, Ben's family had a lot of influence in the area, which would likely make it all disappear if anyone complained.

When everyone returned, they noticed that Anthony's car was there, but he was nowhere to be found. They started to worry as there was no sign of him and Brittany's parents hadn't seen him since before they all left for their big adventure. Everyone took turns calling his cellphone and sending him text messages, but there was no response. Concern began to grow amongst the group, especially with Amanda.

Amanda was freaking out and did the only thing she could think of, call Coach. She quickly informed him of the situation and once again Vincent stopped what he was doing to help Anthony. Vincent was at a New Year's party with Vanessa and some friends, but as soon as he received the phone call, he left to head over to Brittany's. However, this time Vanessa was going with him because she wanted to help.

As Vincent and Vanessa arrived, Amanda informed them that a few of their friends had already gone out looking for Anthony, but they had no word of anyone finding him yet. Vincent immediately grabbed a flashlight from the back of his Jeep and began searching himself.

Since the rest of the group had gone to look throughout the neighborhood, to the school, and to his old house, Vincent began by walking around the house and into the backyard. While back there, he noticed the path that lead through the woods, and realized that nobody had thought to head that way. He began down the path, shinning the light around to see if there were any sign of Anthony or Sammie.

Vincent called out for Anthony over and over again, but there was never a reply. Vincent continued to walk the exact same path that Anthony had traveled two hours earlier, but couldn't find any evidence that he had actually been through there. As Vincent arrived at the clearing, he once again called out Anthony's name. Instead of hearing a voice making a reply, he heard a dog begin to bark. Vincent noticed Sammie running towards him, but there wasn't any sign of Anthony. As he approached Sammie, all he did was take off back to where he had come from. Vincent figured that Sammie knew something that he didn't and instantly began to follow. He walked towards the boxer and found Anthony lying on the ground asleep, next to his parent's grave.

Vincent knelt down next to Anthony and gently woke him up. Anthony was confused at first, but soon realized where he was, that he must have fallen asleep, and that somehow Coach had found him.

The emotions rushed out of him as he began to open up. "Coach, I don't want to be afraid of life anymore. I'm at peace that God had this happen for a reason. I'm sorry for all of the pain I've put you through. You've only been there for me: as a friend, coach, and a second father. Please forgive me for everything I've done!"

Vincent gave Anthony a big hug, "I forgive you, let's just get you back home and warm you up. We have plenty of time to deal with everything."

But Anthony wasn't sure that was the case at all. He had done unthinkable things and acted with a complete lack of respect towards everyone that mattered to him. He just hoped that Coach was right and that he hadn't ruined everything in his life; leaving all of his relationships tattered, broken, and irreconcilable.

Vincent, Anthony, and Sammie walked back through the path to Brittany's house. As they did, Vincent called Amanda to let her know that he found Anthony and to have her contact everyone to call off the search. She was happy that Anthony was alright and she quickly did as Coach asked.

They arrived back at Brittany's house to find some people had already made their way back. Anthony was visibly different than he had been over the past 6 weeks. Like the gravity of the situation had finally sunk in and he was able to release it all. Anthony smiled when he saw Amanda return from searching for him. She looked happy to see that he was alright, but deep down she was saddened that once again he'd done something to put his life in danger, caused problems for others, and made her worry for his safety. Her love for Anthony had never diminished, but their relationship had been seriously strained over all of Anthony's shenanigans. But for now, she was just happy to know that he was safe and looked happier than she'd seen in weeks.

Amanda also witnessed Anthony being kind to Coach Tanzino and everyone else, which made her hopeful that the guy she fell in love with was back. Before they left, Anthony made sure to give Amanda a big hug and a kiss as he told her he loved her and thanked her for always being there for him, even though he'd made things extremely difficult on her. This made her feel better, as this was the nicest he'd been in a while.

After Anthony said his goodbyes, Vincent and Vanessa took him home so that he could sleep off the rest of the alcohol and try to forget how badly the end of 2014 had been for him. Vincent just hoped that Anthony wouldn't relapse into the abyss that he appeared to have returned from and believed this was a good sign that Anthony was finally on the right track and could start 2015 off heading in the right direction.

Chapter Twenty One

New Year – New Beginnings

Thursday: January 1, 2015

Noon came and went, and Anthony hadn't gotten out of bed yet. While, Vincent had already made breakfast for Vanessa, who then left to pick up groceries for the dinner that she planned to make for her and the boys. This left Vincent to get some work done, as he had film to watch and notes to take in preparation for the teams upcoming practices. His notes included a weekly schedule of conditioning, technique and drills intended to fix any deficiencies or enhance their skills, along with live matches amongst the team. His program was comprehensive and elaborate, but extremely effective. Vincent knew that the more effort he put in, the more success that would occur.

Anthony woke up hearing whistles blowing, screaming and yelling, which told him that Vincent was watching film as he regularly did. Anthony remained in bed for a few minutes as he had an excruciatingly painful headache and an upset stomach. He felt awful for what he'd been doing over the past month and a half, but he didn't know how to make up for it. All he thought about was how he'd wasted so many weeks of his senior season drinking, getting into trouble, and causing a rift between him and all of the remaining people in his life that meant anything to him.

Anthony got out of bed and went to his dresser to pull out a pair of sweats that he usually wore during practice. As he threw them on, the excitement and feeling of being a wrestler came rushing back to him as a desire to win filled his thoughts. Anthony looked at a picture of his parents that was sitting on his nightstand, and knew what he had to do. He needed to dedicate the rest of his season and his life in honor of them. He knew that being successful at everything he took on was the only acceptable outcome from now on, but he was still faced with a major problem, how to get back onto the wrestling team.

He knew that he'd have to mend all of the fences that he had broken, especially with Coach.

Anthony left his room and headed downstairs. As he walked into the living room, he saw Coach sitting on the couch watching film.

Vincent noticed him entering the living room and paused the match that he was watching, "Morning, how are you feeling?"

"Like crap," admitted Anthony.

Vincent smiled as he knew how awful it felt to be hungover. But, at least Anthony was being nice to him and not yelling, which he took as a good sign that he wouldn't revert back to how he'd been acting lately. "It's nice to see you wearing workout clothes. I haven't seen that in a while."

"It feels good," stated Anthony. He took a moment before adding, "Coach, I'm really sorry for everything I put you through. I know I've been a handful." As he talked, tears began to form in Anthony's eyes as a dejected feeling engulfed him.

"Anthony, it's okay. You were grieving and you didn't know how to handle all of your feelings." Vincent got up to give Anthony a hug, which he openly embraced.

Anthony held on tight as he began to cry. They sat there hugging one another for a few minutes before Anthony let go and began to open up, "It still doesn't account for what I've done."

Vincent knew there were a lot of obstacles that Anthony would have to overcome, but he'd be right there with him the entire way. For now, Vincent needed to comfort Anthony and let him know just how much he cared and that everything would be alright. "People understand how hard this has been on you. Just know that I forgive you and so does everyone else."

"Are you sure? I think I've really screwed up. I want to wrestle again, but I know that I've pissed everyone off, including you. Besides, I'm out of shape and overweight which will make it difficult for me to get back down to 160."

Without any hesitation, Vincent stated, "I'll allow you back, if the team accepts you joining them again. You'll have to ask them to forgive you and if they want you back on the team. You let them down, so you're going to have to get their trust back."

"That's fair. I knew I'd have to do something. Can I meet them before practice tomorrow and talk to them?" asked Anthony, as he was ready to face the consequences of his actions.

"I'll do one better, I'm having everyone meet here in about an hour for a team film session."

"Everyone?" questioned Anthony, as he was a bit shocked that he didn't have much time to figure out how to convince everyone to give him a second chance.

"Yes, everyone," replied Vincent.

"I guess I better get ready," stated Anthony as he quickly headed back upstairs to his room.

Anthony spent the next hour writing down everything he wanted to say to his teammates. He wrote five pages of notes, even though he knew he wouldn't look at those pages while he spoke to them, but he felt as though he needed to put everything down in writing to organize his thoughts. Anthony remained in his room as the team arrived. Most of them joked around and talking about their New Year's Eve, or lack thereof, as the time approached for the meeting to begin.

Coach Tanzino began to speak, "I'm glad you all agreed to meet at my place for this emergency meeting."

"Coach what's this about, aren't we just going to watch film?" asked Tim.

"It's going to be a little bit more than that today," replied Vincent.

This confused the team. With concern in his voice, Tim asked, "Is something wrong Coach? You're not leaving us are you? Don't tell us that big college offer finally came your way."

"I have someone that'll tell you guys everything for me," Vincent explained before he called out, "Anthony you can come down now."

The team was surprised to see Anthony. Most of them hadn't either seen or spoken with him since he quit. Some began to smile, anticipating his return, while others were angered that he'd show his face and want to talk to them after what he'd done to the team. Even though they'd gone undefeated and won every tournament since he quit, it was more difficult than it should have been had Anthony been there.

Coach saw the look on their faces and made sure to help give Anthony the benefit of the doubt, "Okay everyone, I know this is a little bit of a shock to you, but just hear him out. Please keep an open mind and don't judge him before he has a chance to explain everything."

Anthony stood there for a minute before nervously uttering anything to his peers, which was out of the ordinary, as he'd never before felt nervousness around his teammates. "Thanks Coach. I wanted the opportunity to first and foremost apologize to each and every one of you for my erratic behavior over the past month and a half. I've been a jerk, disrespectful, and downright an asshole. I know I let you all down, but nobody's more disappointed in me than myself. I not only let you down as teammates, but also as friends. I wasn't being the leader that I was supposed to be, I was just thinking about myself and how unfair life had been.

"I turned away and ignored those that meant so much to me and were only trying to help me out in my time of need. You all stood by while my parents were being buried, but I was quick to remove you all from my life. I know I don't deserve to be completely forgiven, but I hope one day I can earn your trust back and hopefully that'll begin today. I'm asking for you all to determine my fate. I'd like to be allowed back on the team, not as a leader or a captain, but as a wrestler. This sport has meant so much and been so good to me, so please allow me the ability to earn back your trust and friendships. I want to dedicate the rest of this season and my life to my parents, but I need your acceptance to move on with the life that I quickly ruined.

"I'm sorry for everything that I did to each of you and I hope you can forgive me and give me one last chance to prove to you that I'm the same guy you've always known and spent countless hours sweating and bleeding with each and every one of you. And I'd like to give a special apology and thanks to Coach for putting up with me and pulling me out of the gutter. I'm truly sorry."

Coach Tanzino liked what he heard as Anthony admitted his wrongdoings and would accept whatever fate his team determined. Vincent then addressed the team, "Guys, you may take some time to discuss this amongst yourselves. Anthony will go into the other room so that you can have your privacy with the decision."

Tim immediately interjected, "Coach, Anthony shouldn't go anywhere. He needs to hear this discussion, not just the verdict."

"Okay, as you wish," agreed Coach Tanzino, as he felt that this might be good for Anthony to hear.

After Anthony's departure from the team, Tim took over as head captain, so it was his team to lead in this upcoming decision. There were many mixed emotions amongst them. Some thought that he'd be a great addition to strengthen their roster and help reach their goal of being conference and state champions. On the other hand, some believed that Anthony coming back to the team would set a bad example and possibly harm what the team was working towards. Anthony had stepped on many toes since the funeral, which left some wrestlers skeptical.

In the end, Dante, his former backup, and current starting 160 pound wrestler, convinced the remainder of the team to let Anthony back. Dante admitted that Anthony wrestling at 160 was the best option for the team. He was happy to step aside and allow Anthony the chance to prove himself.

As a condition to returning to the team, Anthony wouldn't be treated like a senior leader, but as an unprivileged wrestler who had to put in the time doing the grunt work like mopping the mats, carrying the medical kit, water cooler and bottles, as well as not getting back the two lockers that he previously had. He'd also have to wrestle Dante off for the starting spot, as nobody was placed into the starting lineup without earning it.

After they'd determined all of his consequences, Tim asked, "Anthony can you accept the terms and conditions of your return?"

Anthony quickly and emphatically replied, "Yes I can!"

This pleased everyone as they felt it was a fair punishment for what he'd done, but that he had earned a second chance. Tim added, "Well, you've got your second chance."

A huge smile formed across Anthony's face, "Thank you guys, you won't regret it!"

He went around hugging and shaking his teammates' hands. He knew that he'd just been given a new lease on life and was extremely grateful for it.

Anthony was filled with happiness, but soon realized that the real challenge was still ahead of him. Now he had to return to the shape that he'd been in before he quit, along with substantiating to everyone that they were right for letting him back on the team. He had so much to prove to everyone, especially his parents who he felt would be watching from above.

Anthony knew they'd be happy that he was dedicating himself to the sport that made all of them so happy throughout the last four years of his life. The sport that had allowed him to travel across the United States and compete against the best that wrestling had to offer. And Anthony thought what better prize than to achieve success in honor of his parents; not only as a wrestler, but in all aspects of his life.

His parents would've wanted him to continue on and achieve the goals that he had before they passed away. He was now at peace with everything that had happened. He missed his parents, but knew that they still lived on in his thoughts and in his heart. He was thankful that God had given him seventeen years with them and was honored to dedicate the rest of his days to their memory.

Chapter Twenty Two

Anthony Returns

Friday: January 2, 2015

Anthony spent the entire day anticipating his first practice back. He dealt with some of the issues that he'd caused with his teachers, but mainly spent his time thinking about getting back on the mat. As the school day came to an end, the team met in Coach Tanzino's room for study hall, like they'd done all season long. As usual, the list of daily jobs was on the board and under mopping the mats was Anthony's name.

Usually seniors were exempt from pre-practice duties, but Coach Tanzino thought it would be appropriate to show the team, and Anthony, that he's back for everyone, not just himself. This was a humbling experience for Anthony, but he accepted his duty and left to get dressed early so that he could sweep and mop the mats prior to practice starting. This was a great opportunity for Anthony to spend some time in the practice room by himself for the first time in a month and a half.

At first, Anthony just stood silently, looking at the pictures, the records, the mat, and every minor detail and smell that presented itself to him. It felt the same, yet oddly different. This time, he had a higher purpose to his career. It was more than just wins and losses; it was about his parents and the future that they'd want for him.

After changing into a pair of sweats, he began to take care of the mats and preparing the room for the upcoming grueling practice. As he was finishing, the room began to fill up with wrestlers anticipating the challenging workout ahead of them and the beginning of the second half of their season, which was laden with Mid-West Conference opponents and post-season competition.

Everyone was already on the mat as Coach Tanzino blew his whistle to start practice. The team began running around the room in a big circle while they awaited further commands from Coach. The team was like a well-oiled machine as they worked diligently through the warm-up. Each wrestler was already covered in sweat as Coach called out further instructions for drills that they'd have to complete. Coach Tanzino made sure to push the wrestlers while they were tired, helping them to learn how to dig deep inside and to push through difficult situations in matches as their muscles fatigued. He hoped this would aid them in the event of finding themselves in overtime.

After warm-ups, Coach Tanzino had the team begin to drill neutral moves. He continued to call out takedowns with specific set-ups, which the team drilled on command. Everyone, except for Anthony, seemed crisp as they drilled a variety of takedowns prior to working on top and bottom moves. Many of the top moves were completed in a series as a means to teach them to string together sets of back points instead of just getting one set of points at a time. Coach knew that the more his team drilled a move, the more likely they'd become second nature, allowing everyone to just react in any situation that arose while in a match.

It was evident that Anthony hadn't been on a mat for a while as his moves didn't flow as well as they once had. The layoff had reduced some of his quickness and his ability to complete each move with an elite skill level. After the team completed their drills, Anthony felt extremely out of shape and somewhat dejected, which wasn't a good sign, since they hadn't even made it to live wrestling yet.

After the teams' second water break, the wrestlers were placed into four man shark groups. The shark group consisted of one wrestler going live against the other three members of the group in a row. Each member would number themselves one, two, three, and four. Then the number one wrestler would wrestle the athlete who was number two, then three, and then four. Then the number two wrestler would go in the middle and take on numbers three, four, and then one. This continued until each wrestler stayed in for the entire rotation and had a chance to wrestle each member of his group a few times. The purpose was to tire out the wrestler in the middle as they faced fresh opponents with different skill sets, which was a tool that was very effective in preparing each athlete for the numerous rigors and challenges that they'd face in any given competition.

Anthony decided to go as the number one wrestler in his group, like he'd always done. By the end of his first live go, it was evident how out of shape he was, but he continued to fight his way through the tiredness, soreness, and pain to finish his rotation. He learned long ago from Coach Tanzino that you never let your opponent see how tired you are, because they'll look at it as a sign of weakness. But today, Anthony was unable to completely hide his lack of energy. After his third live go, he managed to make his way to the water cooler, where he sat with a water bottle, guzzling fluids, until it was his turn to go again.

Even though Anthony was tired and out of shape, he had experienced a successful practice up to this point as he wrestled well against everyone. He was able to take his teammates down, but not with the same vigor, ability, and ease that he once had. Anthony wasn't as crisp or nearly as quick as he had previously been, but his drive and determination was back with a vengeance.

His aggressive nature on the mat, combined with his knowledge, and his desire to return to the sport that he loved proved to be beneficial tools throughout his first practice back. Anthony may not have been in shape, but his knowledge and experiences hadn't diminished. Instead, he knew that he'd have to rely heavily on them until he improved his conditioning to where it needed to be.

After wrestling through the shark groups, Coach Tanzino paired up members of the team, and placed 10 minutes on the clock as each duo would wrestle live for the entire time. Coach periodically stopped the match to give each wrestler a fresh start in different positions; otherwise, they didn't have a chance to rest. Coach Tanzino placed Anthony with Tim, his biggest competition, right away. Coach knew that if Anthony was going to get back to where he'd previously been, he needed to challenge him each step of the way.

The battle ensued between these two fierce competitors. But Tim's conditioning proved to be a major factor throughout the entire match, yet Anthony never gave up and fought for the entire 10 minutes. Each athlete was extremely familiar with the others' strengths and weaknesses, which always made for a challenging match in practice. Both of them had glimpses of success against the other, as they earned takedowns, reversals, escapes, and even near fall points.

As the 10 minutes ended, Anthony was extremely winded as he did everything he could to get more air into his lungs. He immediately knew that if they'd kept score, that Tim would have beaten him, which was the first time that had ever happened. The matches used to be close and challenging, yet Tim was never able to beat the more talented wrestler.

It was evident that Anthony was thinking about this as he sat in the corner of the room, with his head in his hands. When he put his head up, a dejected look appeared on his face, as he thought about how much he'd lost. Sadly, it only had taken six weeks of inactivity and partying to ruin years of constant training.

However, Anthony didn't have a lot of time to dwell on his fatigue against Tim, as the team went through two more 10 minute goes. Anthony was pitted against Coach Tanzino in the second match and Dante in the third. Anthony was unable to compete with Vincent, as his years of experience and physical fitness were too much to handle. This wasn't unusual for Vincent to beat Anthony, but it had been a couple of years since he had done so with such ease. But, Anthony finally saw a glimpse of success as he beat Dante handily throughout their entire go. It wasn't much, but it was still a confidence booster for Anthony, as he was able to end the live portion of the practice on a high note, even though he was exhausted.

Once the matches were over, the team immediately did a set of sprawls, a set of 30 second shots, along with more push-ups, sit-ups, and sprints. The object of making them complete these drills right after wrestling three live goes was to enhance their conditioning while forcing them to work on their technique while fatigued. This not only pushed their physical abilities, but their mental toughness as well.

As practice came to an end, Tim led the team in stretching. A job that once belonged to Anthony, but was no longer his. But, he didn't mind, Anthony was just happy to be back in the room and back on a wrestling mat. In-spite of the challenges the day had presented to him, he felt honored to be going through the grind once again. He'd been through a lot since the last time he'd done so, but now it was different. Anthony had a higher purpose to his season and his life, and a lack of conditioning wasn't going to stop him from achieving his goals.

Afterwards, everyone but Anthony went to the locker room to shower after practice to prevent ringworm and various other skin irritations. Anthony sat on the mat, drenched in sweat, and getting the air back into his lungs before making his way to the Coach Tanzino's office for a meeting to discuss his first day back. While in the meeting, Anthony broke down and began to cry as the emotions bubbled to the surface in his first experience with wrestling since his parents passed away. Coach was extremely supportive and happy to see Anthony letting out some of his feelings. Vincent knew that in time it would get easier on him, but for now, showing positive signs of emotion would aid in his recovery.

Even though he was happy to be back, Anthony was still somewhat disappointed. He opened up and talked to Coach Tanzino about how difficult it was to be back on the mat, knowing how much he'd lost in such a short period of time. Vincent let Anthony say whatever was on his mind, as he knew that he'd have to be Anthony's spring board. Vincent was just glad that the old Anthony was back, as he hadn't talked to him like this since the accident, and it had been severely missed.

After Anthony finished talking, Vincent explained that there'd be plenty of hard times to come, but to stick with it and fight through those demanding and disconcerting days. Vincent also promised to be there for him and to help provide additional opportunities for Anthony to get back into shape. This seemed to have a positive effect on Anthony, as it made him feel a little better because he knew that Coach was on his side and would be there every step of the way.

The locker room had cleared out by the time Anthony took his shower. He was glad as he wanted to be alone with his thoughts. It had been a long time since he was on a mat, and he'd missed it, but it was a difficult first day back. Yet, Anthony was confident that it would only get easier over the coming weeks. He was just going to have to grit and bare it, digging deep inside of himself for the ability to succeed.

When Anthony and Vincent returned home, they were greeted by the wonderful smell of food and a smiling Vanessa. She wanted to have dinner made for them when they returned home. Since Anthony had begun his diet, he only had a small bite to eat and then immediately went to bed. The first day was not totally what Anthony had expected, but it was only the beginning, and exactly what he needed to bring some normalcy back to his life.

Once Anthony had gone up to his room, Vincent informed Vanessa about Anthony's first day back to practice and just how difficult it had been on him. She was concerned and wanted to know how she could be of assistance. Vincent thought for a minute, and then told her to be ready to keep certain foods out of the house and to be prepared that Anthony might be irritable from cutting weight over the next few weeks. Plus for her to be supportive and encouraging like a parent or a big sister would be. Vincent knew that Anthony needed as much help in those areas from as many people as possible. And he knew that Vanessa's caring nature and understanding of what it took to be a successful athlete would only aid in Anthony's recovery.

Besides, Vincent knew that he'd need her continued support, as this would be difficult and draining on him as well. There were many long hours ahead of them as he knew there was only a short period of time for Anthony to get back into shape and ready to take on athletes who had been training all along, and hadn't taken weeks off in the middle of the season. This could prove to be a significant disadvantage for Anthony, but Vincent was going to do everything in his power to prevent it from derailing their ultimate goal of a state championship.

January 3-16, 2015

As the days turned into two weeks of practice, Anthony began to gain back some of the steps that he'd lost over his hiatus. His matches with Tim began to even out, but he was still unable to match skills with

Vincent, which he truly hadn't been able to do prior to taking time off, but had been a lot closer than he currently was.

The team had wrestled and been victorious in three conference duals and one tournament throughout his two weeks back, but Anthony hadn't wrestled yet. He needed to first make weight and secondly get into better shape. Vincent didn't want Anthony to wrestle a match until the time was right, which he felt was rapidly approaching. Their target for his return was the match against the South Hills Cougars, the reigning 7-time Mid-West Conference Champions. It would be the perfect challenge for Anthony, besides, the team would need him if they had a chance to come away with a victory.

Anthony took every possible opportunity he could to workout. He began waking up early and getting a run in prior to school. He took advantage of his Gym class by spending time in the weight room gaining back some of his strength, while toning up. He also asked for help from Vincent and some of his teammates by having them stay after practice for additional mat time. All of these measures were slowly, but surely allowing Anthony to make the necessary recovery and gains needed for him to be successful in his attempt at retuning to the level of competition that he was accustom to producing.

Even though Anthony had only taken six weeks off, those weeks were spent eating everything in sight and consuming a tremendous amount of alcohol. Anthony was amazed at how quickly someone could get out of shape, considering it took so long to get into shape. He realized that it wouldn't be easy, but his heart and his mind were in the right place for the first time in weeks and he was dedicated to making everything right.

Anthony wanted to do whatever was necessary to honor his parents. He felt that pushing himself to his limits and beyond was the only way that he could do so. He knew that his parents would be watching him and helping him from above as his return to wrestling was not only for himself, but for them as well. He felt as though his parents deserved for him to give everything he had, as they had done the same for him throughout his entire life.

The training was not the only aspect of Anthony's life that needed to be fixed. He'd slacked on his classwork and his grades had suffered significantly. He needed to spend extra time making up all of his missed assignments and retaking tests. Vincent talked to each of Anthony's teachers, who were willing to take some of his late assignments and have him retake tests as long as he attended class and did everything they asked of him. The teachers were very understanding of Anthony's predicament, so they agreed to do as much as they could because they wanted to show how much they cared for him. As Anthony's grades improved, so did his health. He was getting back into shape and properly losing weight in the process.

The only thing left was to fix his relationship with Amanda, who showed him nothing but love throughout his time of need. However, he had taken advantage of her love and her kindness; things that he'd have to earn back. Anthony became the best man possible to her because his parents had taught him to be that way. He opened doors for her, and carried her books while they were in school. He showed her just how much he loved her and appreciated all that she'd done while he was mourning his parents' death.

Everyone seemed happy to see the old Anthony back, but nobody more than Vincent. He had held things together for Anthony the best he could throughout those dark days. Vincent put out the fires as much as possible while trying to keep colleges interested in him and teachers off his back. Vincent did what he knew was in Anthony's best interest, even if Anthony wasn't aware of it or realized what was the right thing to do at the time. Vincent knew that Anthony would regret it if he never returned or flunked out of high school, because the Williams' highly valued his education and his athletic career. They knew that there was something special about their son and they wanted nothing but success for him in his future, which ultimately why they worked so hard to provide a life that they could've only dreamt of as they were growing up.

Anthony knew how lucky he'd been for everything that his parents had given up for him, which was why he was working so hard to come back from the mess that he had placed himself in. Anthony felt that his actions needed to always reflect his desire to honor them.

He also wanted to be as close to them as possible at all times. This caused Anthony to place something special inside his headgear to constantly remind him that his parents would always be there with him. Now the only thing left was to make weight and begin competing against other teams; a challenge that Anthony finally felt ready for.

Chapter Twenty Three

The Parkside Mustangs
– vs –
The South Hill Cougars

Tuesday: January 20th, 2015

The day of Anthony's first match back brought a whirlwind of publicity to the wrestlers, especially Anthony; however, he tried to ignore everyone and focus on his match, leaving Coach Tanzino to deal with the publicity. The anticipation was enormous as the Mustang faithful thought that there wouldn't be enough seats for everyone, leading many to plan to get there early to guarantee a place in the stands. Once the team had rolled out the mats, Coach Tanzino gathered them together as he wanted to discuss a few things.

"I need to briefly talk to you guys. I know you've been asked questions all day long, which might have gotten some of you distracted from tonight's match. But, if we can win tonight, we take the conference lead and possibly take the title away from the South Hill Cougars for the first time in nearly a decade. We need to remain focused on the task at hand, not the media frenzy that'll be present. This match was already going to be big, but with Anthony's return, and so many guys on both sides ranked in the state, it just might be the biggest any of you have been in. Just remain focused and leave the media, the fans, and everything else to me. No one talk to anyone from the minute we go back to get weighed in until the minute we shake hands to end the match, got it?"

Everyone shook their heads in agreement, while others answered, "Yes Coach."

"Good, is there anything we need to talk about before people are allowed in here?" asked Vincent.

Even though Vincent didn't want to talk in front of the crowd, he didn't have a problem having this speech while the cameramen were setting up as the match was going to be aired live on one of the public television stations, an honor that usually was reserved for football or basketball games. However, the enormity of this match and Anthony's return catapulted it to a live broadcast.

Tim felt the need to quickly add, "This is what we've been working so hard for. No one comes into our house and beats us. The pressure is on them to keep us away from their title as we have nothing to lose. So go out there and do what we've been taught to do, dominate our opponents, continue to work, and never give up. Wrestle your match and just win!"

Coach knew that he couldn't have said it any better. He looked around at the young men standing in front of him. There was fire in their eyes as they were ready for whatever was to come. For the first time in his four years as a coach, Vincent knew that his team was ready to dethrone the champions.

The South Hill Cougars showed up right as the crowd was being allowed into the gym. Security had been increased for the match, not only because of the added crowd and the repercussions from the match, but because of the increased media presence as well. This included Officer Bill Robbins, who requested to be on duty for the match as he wanted to show his support for Anthony. Unfortunately for him, he still couldn't get the tragedy of that night out of his mind. It had changed this young man's life forever, but Bill hoped that this was a sign that Anthony was getting his life back on track.

Coach Tanzino immediately went over to Coach Smith, the South Hill's Head Coach, and led him and his team to the scale to allow them to check their weights prior to the official weigh-in. Once the South Hill Cougars were ready, the Mustangs entered the training room, where the scale was and the weigh-ins always occurred. The buzz was growing amongst the South Hill wrestlers that Anthony Williams was back. This was the first time that he'd be back competing, so no one in the area was prepared for his return. There had been rumors, but until he actually stepped foot on the scale, nobody was sure what to believe. This made their 160 pound wrestler realize he was going to have an extremely tough match ahead of him, maybe even the deciding factor in winning or losing the dual meet and gaining a stronghold on the conference championship.

There was a phenomenal amount of wrestling talent standing in the room. Seven wrestlers were ranked in the top five in the state, not including Anthony, who was no longer ranked due to his absence. This clearly made for a must see experience for the fans and a dual meet that the athletes would always remember.

As each wrestler stepped onto the scale, their exact weight was recorded. Everyone did as they were supposed to as weigh-ins went smoothly for both teams. Even Anthony made weight without any serious issues. He was slightly dehydrated from the cut, but nothing that some Gatorade couldn't fix.

It was the Coaches turn to determine where the match would begin and end. Coach Tanzino pulled out a deck of cards, which included the Ace through King of Hearts and the King of Spades, as each represented a weight class. Coach Tanzino showed Coach Smith all of the cards, identified by a weight class, which had been written in the upper left hand corner. Vincent then shuffled the cards and allowed Coach Smith to choose which match would go first. Coach Smith pulled the 10 of hearts, which meant that the 170 pound weight class was first up.

"I guess we left the best match for last," stated Coach Tanzino to Coach Smith.

"Yes we did, 160 should be one hell of a bout if Anthony's ready to make his way back to the mat, if not, he's going to get beat badly by Travis," replied Coach Smith.

This comment put a smile on Vincent's face, as he knew how smug Coach Smith was. And why shouldn't he be, he'd dominated the local competition for years, but to Vincent, tonight felt different. "We'll just have to see Coach."

"Yes we will. Good luck."

"Good luck to you too," replied Vincent as they shook hands.

Both Coach Tanzino and Coach Smith headed their separate ways towards their respective locker rooms. As Vincent entered his teams' locker room, he heard nothing but music being played in his athletes headphones. The team was getting dressed, eating food, and taping their wrestling shoes for the match. They were extremely focused, which Vincent loved to see as he felt this was a good sign for what would occur in less than an hour.

"Alright guys," Coach Tanzino began, "make sure you're ready, because this sets the tone for the remainder of the season. The draw is exactly what we wanted, 170 will be going first, leaving 160 for last. So the crowd's going to get what they want, the most anticipated match will be the last one of the evening. Tim, you can start us off on the right note and Anthony can close the door on the Cougars."

The team didn't say a word; they just nodded their heads in agreement and remained focused. They knew the importance of this match and were prepared to do whatever was necessary to dethrone the champs. The Mustangs had put in countless hours of blood, sweat, and tears to make it to this point and they weren't going to let this opportunity slip away.

There wasn't an empty seat in the gym, forcing some spectators to stand to watch. South Hill's was allowed to warm-up first; in front of the capacity crowd of 3,000. While they were on the mat, the home biased Parkside crowd began to chant "Mustangs" in support of their team. The Cougars had never experienced anything like it as the match hadn't even started and they were feeling the presence of the hostile environment.

Once the Cougars were done warming up, it was time for the Mustangs to take the mat. As the music began to play; the Mustangs came running out of their locker room and onto the mat. The crowd erupted into deafening cheers as the atmosphere was electric, which filled each wrestler with pride. They had never felt anything like this before, which only added to the adrenaline that coursed through their veins. The wrestlers circled the mat and began to warm-up, stretch, and drill their moves, while the music continued to play and the crowd continued to cheer them on.

At the end of the warm-up, the team met in the middle of the mat where Tim led them in the custom pre-match "Our Father," prayer. After they prayed, Tim counted to three and the team beat the mat and screamed Mustangs before they got up and walked to their home bench. They were now just mere moments away from the start of the match.

But first, the captains were asked to come to the center of the mat for the coin toss and the customary pre-match handshake. The official tossed his coin in the air, and as it parachuted down and hit the mat, it landed on green giving Parkside the choice. Coach Tanzino had Tim elect to take the even matches, which meant that South Hill's had to present their wrestler first to the table during the odd matches, while Parkside did so for the even matches. This would continue throughout the fourteen bouts and was a strategy that allowed coaches to bump their wrestlers around to present the best possible line-up to win the dual meet.

Coach Tanzino initially thought that Coach Smith might want his 160 pound wrestler to take his chances against Tim instead of Anthony. But as the first match was set to begin, it was evident that it wasn't his strategy at all. Vincent saw the confidence in Coach Smith's eyes, as he must have felt that Travis could beat Anthony, especially after his two month hiatus from competition. This meant that the match that everyone came to see would actually occur.

The scoreboard operator put the number 170 on the scoreboard; to indicate what match was going to be coming up. At that moment, Tim walked onto the mat, which prompted the crowd to begin to whisper to one another that Anthony's match would be the last one of the evening. This only added another layer of excitement to the capacity crowd as the noise hit new heights on the decibel meter.

Tim took complete control of his opponent from the opening whistle. This gave the home crowd a lot to cheer for as Tim earned a 15-4 major decision giving the Mustangs a four point lead in the team score. Parkside continued its winning ways with a 4-2 decision by Cary Washington at 182 pounds, advancing the team score to 7-0. The Mustangs took their lead into the 195 pound weight class where Roberto Alazar earned a two point victory, giving them three more team points and extended their lead to 10-0.

Everything had gone smoothly for the Mustangs from the onset, but their lead was about to be challenged as the third ranked 220 pound wrestler from South Hill pinned Mike Robinson at the 1:52

mark of the first period. Ryan Thompson, Parkside's eighth ranked Heavyweight, lost in a 7-5 upset, tightening up the team score, as Parkside held a slight 10-9 advantage. But that advantage would soon disappear as the Cougars earned a 7-2 decision at 106 against Matt States and then a pin at 113 against Gary Joseph to extend their lead to 18-10.

Parkside senior Chris States, who was ranked third in the state at 120, wanted to make up for his younger brother's loss. Chris understood that he needed to stop the bleeding and end the teams losing streak if they remotely had a chance at winning the dual meet. He aggressively pursued his opponent and didn't stop until the referee blew his whistle at the end of the match, indicating that Chris had earned a 19-4 technical fall, cutting into the lead as the team score was now 18-15 in favor of the Cougars.

Joe Staley, the Parkside 126 pounder, earned a pin to take back the lead at 21-18, in this see-saw battle. But the advantage was short lived as the South Hill Cougars highly ranked 132 and 138 pound wrestlers both earned pins. This gave the Cougars an almost insurmountable lead at 30-21 with only three matches left. The only way that the Mustangs were guaranteed to earn a victory was if they won all three remaining bouts.

Knowing how important the final three matches were to a Parkside victory, Coach Tanzino pulled Tyron, Antwon, and Anthony together behind the bench. Vincent needed to express his thoughts to them and explain how much their matches meant towards the team beating the Cougars, because even one loss could derail this golden opportunity.

After the speech, the Parkside 145 pound wrestler, Tyron Johnson, took Coach Tanzino's words to heart as he got the ball rolling with a second period pin of his opponent. The Mustangs were now only down 30-27 heading into a match that seemed to doom them. Dean Smith, the fifth ranked wrestler from South Hill, and Coach Smith's son, would likely beat Antwon Jones and solidify their victory.

Antwon would have to wrestle the best match of his career to pull off the upset. He used every bit of knowledge from training with his talented teammates and coaches to his advantage. He knew that no matter what, he couldn't make a mistake. He had to wrestle a flawless match if he was going to give his team a chance for victory.

Antwon found himself fighting off a barrage of shots by Dean, but after a few, he made a less than ideal attempt at a single leg shot, one that Antwon was able to capitalize on as he earned a takedown in the first period. Antwon added an escape in the second period and fortunately for him, he was able to control the pace of the match. His only mistake came late in the match as he gave up a reversal with a few seconds left in the third period. After an extremely hard fought match, Antwon pulled off a major upset with a 3-2 win. Antwon used a defensive strategy to perfection as he kept Dean from using his offense to run up the score. Instead, Antwon capitalized on Dean's aggressive nature, scoring points early and then holding him off for the rest of the match.

The win knotted everything up at 30-30 with one bout to go. If Anthony won, then the Mustangs would win the match, if he didn't, the Cougars would come away victorious.

Anthony had already placed a tremendous amount of pressure on himself, but knowing the outcome was on his shoulders, only added to it. Prior to Anthony's match, Vincent stood behind the bench with him to give his final words of encouragement. Coach noticed how overwhelmingly nervous Anthony appeared, which was uncharacteristic for him. He couldn't recall any point in Anthony's career that he remotely looked like this. Vincent knew that if he didn't find a way to ease some of this pressure, all of his hard work over the past two weeks would've been for nothing.

"What's wrong?" asked Vincent.

"I'm more nervous than I've ever been," admitted Anthony.

"It's okay. You've done this a thousand times. Just go out there and wrestle your match and you can win. You have the knowledge and the experience. Just know that I believe in you, as I always have."

"But Coach, I'm sad because this is the first time I've ever wrestled without at least one of my parents being present."

Vincent knew this might be a problem, but he wanted to reassure this young man who meant so much to him. "Anthony, you'll never wrestle a match without your parents because they're in your heart and in your mind. Just know that they're always watching from Heaven. Besides, I've never missed a match either. Now go out there and show us the magic you have. Just wrestle your match and forget about all of these people because it's just you, your opponent, and your guardian angel on that mat."

Anthony felt a little more confident and a little less nervous after hearing what Coach had to say. Seeing his words had calmed Anthony down, Vincent added, "Now, let's see what you can do!"

At that moment Anthony ran onto the mat in front of a crowd that was filled with mass hysteria. The eruption from them was like no other match that evening. Both teams were cheering for their wrestler, knowing that this bout decided the outcome.

This was it, the match of the night was about to begin and it held the fate of each teams' fortunes. Victory by either wrestler not only meant that they won, but that their team would also come away with the win and likely the conference championship. The competitors and their teams weren't the only ones aware of this fact as the entire crowd knew it as well. The referee had both wrestlers stand on their respective lines and shake hands. He moved away and blew his whistle, signaling the beginning of the match.

Travis immediately began an offensive onslaught against Anthony. Travis' plan was to get Anthony winded to hopefully capitalize on his lack of conditioning. Travis knew that the layoff from competition would be in his favor as Anthony hadn't wrestled anyone other than his teammates, since November. Travis hoped that the rumors had been true about how much weight Anthony had gained from all of the partying that he'd done and that his time off made him rusty. Besides, this wasn't the first time they'd wrestled each other, and since most of the other matches had been close, Travis hoped that Anthony's time off would give him a slight edge.

Travis was the aggressor as he took a few shots on Anthony, who was able to defend his first two attempts; however, the third, a sweep single, was too many for the slowed down athlete. Travis grabbed Anthony's left leg, lifted it up, causing Anthony to become off balanced, while still trying to defend the takedown attempt. The South

Hill's wrestler continued to lift the leg all the way to his right shoulder, where he followed it up by sweeping Anthony's right leg from underneath him, causing him to fall to his stomach on the mat.

Two fingers were raised up by the referee, indicating that Travis was in the lead 2-0 after earning a takedown. Anthony fought hard, but nothing seemed to free him from Travis' grip. Travis eventually locked up a bar arm and tilted Anthony as time ran out. Two more points were awarded to Travis as he had earned a two point near fall.

The scoreboard read 4-0 after the first in Travis' favor. Anthony was angered at his lack of control of the match. It was Anthony's period to choose top, down, neutral, or to defer. Anthony looked at Coach Tanzino, who indicated for Anthony to defer his option to get what he wanted at the beginning of the third, instead of in the second. Once the option was his, without hesitation, Travis chose down so that he could try to earn an escape or a reversal and pad his lead.

It took nearly 30 seconds before Travis earned his escape, and one more point. Now he had a sizeable 5-0 lead over Anthony, who didn't look like he had any chance to work his way out of this deficit. Both Travis and Anthony were setting up shots, but neither was successful at taking the other one down. After going out of bounds, with only 20 seconds left in the period, both Anthony and Coach Tanzino knew something had to be done. By this point, Anthony couldn't hear the cheers coming from the crowd or his teammates. The only voice he heard was Coach Tanzino's telling him to grab a Russian tie and go for a high crotch or an inside trip. Vincent had noticed that Travis was starting to get tired and lazy with his tie-ups and footwork.

As the whistle blew, Anthony stepped towards Travis, which prompted him to reach with his right hand, placing it on the back of Anthony's head. Anthony immediately did as Coach wanted him to and grabbed a Russian tie. Within seconds he had already hit an inside trip, making Travis fall directly to his back, where Anthony was able to hold him for three seconds before he bellied out and remained until the second period came to an end. Anthony had just earned two points for the takedown and another two points for the near fall.

Now only down 5-4, entering the third period, Anthony had built up a little confidence that he could win this match. Anthony looked over to Coach Tanzino who told him to pick down. Anthony listened to his coach and quickly got in the bottom position. With only two minutes left, Anthony knew that he had to do something, but he struggled to get any points for the first minute and a half of the period. Once again the two competitors' action forced them out of bounds, giving Anthony a much needed fresh start. Coach Tanzino kept screaming for Anthony to move immediately on the whistle, as time was running out for him to score points.

Anthony was set in the down position as Travis slowly got on top. All of a sudden, Anthony felt a burst of energy at the exact moment that the referee blew his whistle. Anthony shot up like a rocket and freed himself of Travis' powerful mitts. This earned Anthony one point for an escape, knotting the score up at five points apiece. Both wrestlers attempted safe shots so that they didn't make a mistake and let the time run out of the period. The score was deadlocked at 5-5, sending the match into overtime. It was fitting that the bout to determine which team would come out victorious needed extra time, which exacerbated the drama of the entire situation.

One minute was placed on the clock as both wrestlers got situated in the neutral position as they were well aware that a takedown would end the match. Both competitors battled throughout the overtime period; however, neither was successful at earning a clinching point.

Time ran out on the sudden victory period, forcing a second overtime consisting of two ride-out periods. The referee gave Travis the first choice as he'd earned the first points in the match. Travis chose down to try and earn an escape or a reversal for a lead prior to the second ride out period. Travis fought hard, but Anthony dug deep as he used a collar tie along with a spiral ride and forward pressure to continue to keep Travis at bay, and prevent him from earning any points during the first 30 seconds.

This left the score tied and gave Anthony a distinct advantage as he chose down for the second 30 second ride out period. All he'd have to do is score more points in the last 30 seconds to earn a victory. As he got set in the bottom position, Anthony looked at

Coach Tanzino who was shouting encouraging words. Anthony was determined to score points by any means necessary. He needed this victory; a victory not only for himself, but for the team that he'd let down for most of the season.

Anthony summoned up every drop of energy that he had left and as the seconds ticked down to ten, Anthony nearly earned a reversal, but with it, he caused enough separation between himself and Travis that with two seconds left, Anthony stood up and earned an escape. As the final seconds ticked off the clock, the Mustangs exploded into cheers, but they weren't even audible over the eruption of the Parkside fans. The roar of the crowd was deafening, but well deserved after the battle of titans had just taken place.

Anthony won the match, giving the Mustangs a 33-30 victory over the seven time defending conference champions, solidifying their place atop the Mid-West Conference standings and in the driver's seat for a conference championship.

After shaking hands with their opponents, the Mustangs mingled with the crowd and broke down the mats before being sent into the locker room to get showered up and have a team meeting once Coach Tanzino was done with his interviews. Anthony didn't even stay in the gym with everyone else. He immediately went into the locker room where he collapsed to the ground from exhaustion. His teammates feed him water and Gatorade as he remained on the ground, trying to recover from the exhilarating match that he'd just participated in.

As Anthony sat on the ground getting rehydrated, tears began to trickle down his face as the emotion of it all hit him. They were tears of joy and sorrow as he felt good to be back on the mat, but sad because his parents weren't physically there to cheer him on. Yet he felt confident that they'd given him the energy necessary to pull off the victory, not only for him, but for those that he'd let down.

While the team showered up and awaited the meeting, Coach Tanzino spoke to the media. "On paper, South Hill's was supposed to win the match, but matches are won or lost on the mat, not on paper. We were determined to win and take control of our fate in regards to a conference championship. We're the first conference team to beat them in more than seven years, which is quite a task considering this is one of their best teams to date. I'm so proud of my team's efforts and determination to pull off such a historic victory for our program."

Coach Tanzino continued to answer questions, which were mostly about Anthony's return. Vincent knew the sensitive nature of the events that had transpired over the past two months, so he didn't give them too many details. Vincent talked about a young man's challenge of overcoming a major tragedy in his life and his ability to find solace in the sport he loves. Coach added that Anthony's return was an indication that normalcy was coming back for a young man who had been dealing with a tragedy that Vincent hoped nobody else would have to ever go through. He continued to speak with them for almost 15 minutes as this victory may have indicated a changing of the guard and a new powerhouse in North Carolina.

At the end, Coach Tanzino thanked the media for being respectful of Anthony's situation as he wanted all requests or questions for the remainder of the season to be asked of him only. As he finished up with the interviews and headed towards the locker room, Coach Tanzino was congratulated one more time, by the media and the remaining fans, for his victory over the perennial conference foe.

He was clearly enjoying the moment as a huge smile engulfed Vincent's face as he entered the locker room that housed his team. Cheers erupted immediately upon his entrance. He congratulated his team prior to reminding them that there was plenty left to accomplish. This was only one step in reaching their ultimate goal of a state championship, but he knew that it was a huge step in the right direction.

Coach Tanzino wanted everyone to enjoy the victory that evening, but to be prepared to get back to work the next day, as they still had plenty of work to do. Vincent knew that he needed to sit back and enjoy the moment, as four years of hard work had culminated in a major accomplishment. This victory had come from endless hours of preparation and hard work. It was the most significant victory thus far in his career as a Coach, and he only hoped there were many more like it on the horizon. Vincent planned to enjoy it that night, before refocusing the next day on the task at hand; earning conference and state championships.

Chapter Twenty Four

Regional Championships

February 9-14, 2015

The week of the regional championships was one filled with excitement for the Parkside Mustangs. They just capped off an undefeated dual team record on the season and with it a dual team state championship. Throughout the previous ten days, the Mustangs had dominated their competition, earning the Mid-West Conference Championship in both the dual season as well as the conference tournament, along with the 2015 North Carolina 4A State Dual Team Championship.

They had handily defeated all of their dual team opponents, demolishing the Lake Norman Lancers and the Davidson Bulldogs in the first two rounds of the dual tournament. They followed it up by dismantling the West Seneca Indians prior to once again beating the East High Eagles in the semi-finals, who themselves had reached that point by narrowly defeating the South Hill Cougars in the previous round. In the state championship match, the Mustangs took a commanding lead against the North Wilmington Warriors and never looked back as they won in an impressive fashion by the final of 35-12 to solidify their perfect season and a state championship.

The 40-0 record was the best for any team in North Carolina at any level and brought about much praise around the state and even nationally. In-spite of the excitement for a triumphant team championship, Coach Tanzino didn't want the Mustangs to focus too long on it. He wanted them to remain determined to achieve their personal goals. Besides, Coach knew that they'd have plenty of time to celebrate all of the seasons' accomplishments in two weeks after the individual state tournament.

On Monday, February 9th, Coach Tanzino had a quick team meeting prior to starting their daily practice routine. The wrestlers met in the practice room and sat on the mats for a brief conversation. Once the entire team was ready and waiting, Coach Tanzino began to speak, "Alright guys, I'd like to congratulate each of you one last time on winning the dual team state championships on Saturday. I'm extremely proud of all of you and I truly appreciate the hard work that you've put into this season thus far. This is the first state championship as a team for this program and I'm so proud of what each of you did to contribute to all of us reaching that goal.

"Now that I've said that, you can celebrate that in a couple of weeks once the individual season comes to an end. It's time to refocus and achieve your personal goals on the season. Many of you wanted to place at regionals and qualify for states, while others wanted to win regionals and states. But, you can't accomplish those goals if you're still thinking about what we did in the past. You need to concentrate all of your energy on the next two weeks and what lies ahead for us. Do you all understand?"

Everyone on the team nodded their heads as they clearly understood that they couldn't rest on what they've already done, but needed to push themselves to accomplish even more. Coach continued, "This week we're getting ready for regionals and that's what has to be your main focus. Each of you needs to push yourself to improve over the next few days, because all of us have an area or two that needs to be worked on. Nobody completely dominated without errors throughout the dual team championships. So, I'm challenging each of you to spend the appropriate amount of time working to fix those mistakes so that you don't make them again."

Each wrestler was completely fixated on each word that Vincent spoke. They obviously understood the magnitude of the situation along with what was being asking of them. By now, the team had gained a real grasp of how things worked; the practices on Monday and Tuesday would be extremely challenging, prior to Coach easing off on Wednesday and Thursday. Coach didn't want them to be too tired or sore by the time they wrestled their first match on Friday afternoon. But Coach also wanted to make sure that he continued to keep them in shape, their weight under control, and their minds focused on the ultimate prize.

Wrestling is one of the most physical sports around, but the mental part of it is even more of a challenge. The concept that each athlete needed to mentally prepare just as hard as they physically prepared was a major aspect of the program that Coach Tanzino wanted to run. Throughout all of his experiences, he knew that the best way to win was having the belief that you can win. If someone goes into a match thinking they'll lose, then most likely they will. And that was unacceptable for the Parkside Mustangs.

As the week progressed, it was evident that each athlete was dedicating themselves to finishing the season on a high note. Coach Tanzino was getting every ounce of energy and desire out of his athletes on and off of the mat. They had thanked everyone for the many congratulations for their dual team championship, but they'd always turn the conversation and the emphasis right back to the regional championships coming up that weekend. Their mental training and focus hadn't waivered throughout the season, and this week was no different. The team believed in what Coach preached and did as was expected, not only for their benefit, but for all that Vincent had done for them and the program. Each wrestler was honored to have Coach Tanzino on their side and they wanted to show him just how appreciative they were.

Wednesday: February 11, 2015

Following practice on Wednesday, Vincent and his assistant coaches drove to the seeding meeting, which was being held at Saint Joe's High School, where the regional championships were taking place. They drove with Coach Tanzino and made the hour and a half trek to the meeting. Once they arrived, they were feed and given the materials on who'd be seeded at what place, according to the pre-seeding information sent in by each of the coaches.

The regional championships were a pre-seeded tournament based on the wrestlers overall record for the entire season. Each coach was required to send in their athletes' records two days earlier so that the tournament seeding meeting could move quickly, instead of being a long arduous process. Then, the records would be turned into win percentages and each wrestler would be seeded accordingly. In the case of a tie, the tie breaker would go to who won in a head-to-head meeting. However, if they hadn't wrestled each other, then it would be a coin flip that determined the higher seed.

Coach Tanzino was confident in the fact that his wrestlers would be highly seeded as the majority of his fourteen starters had great overall season records, even after taking on the best competition in and out of the state of North Carolina.

While there, many of the other coaches congratulated Coach Tanzino and his coaching staff on winning a state championship. Vincent was grateful to be getting such praise from his competitors and colleagues. He'd put a tremendous amount of effort into making it to this point and the dedication had finally paid off with a team championship, but to Vincent, it wasn't enough. He never had any of his wrestlers win a North Carolina individual state championship and he wanted that to change and Vincent knew he had a few wrestlers that could accomplish that goal this season. Unfortunately, many people wouldn't include Anthony as one of them, but Vincent knew otherwise.

The Parkside coaching staff was pleased at the way that the team was seeded, since they had six wrestlers slotted into one of the top four spots in their respective weight classes, while all fourteen wrestlers were able to qualify, which wasn't an automatic occurrence. Since the West Regional had 26 teams and each weight class was based on a sixteen man bracket, it was possible that ten wrestlers per weight class wouldn't even make it into the tournament.

Seeing that every one of their wrestlers would be taking the trip to wrestle that weekend, the Parkside coaching staff congratulated one another. But Vincent didn't dwell on the fact that they made it into the tournament, he began thinking about how each of his athletes could win the tournament. He knew it would be difficult, but Vincent was confident in the work that each of his athletes had put in. He believed that it was realistic for seven or eight of the guys to qualify for states the following weekend, anything above that would be icing on the cake. Even knowing that half of his team would likely qualify, he wanted all of them to make it, as they'd worked hard enough throughout the season and were deserving of a chance at the ultimate prize.

The seeding meeting progressed to the 160 pound weight class. Anthony was awarded the 7-seed, meaning that he might have to wrestle the top three competitors in his weight class to win the tournament or even just to qualify for the state championships. Even though Anthony went into the regional tournament with an 11-0 record, according to the rules, each wrestler was seeded off of a fifteen match minimum, meaning that any match below the minimum would be counted as a loss on the athlete's record. This left Anthony to be seeded off of an 11-4 record, and a 0.73 win percentage, instead of the perfect record that he had earned. This unfortunate ruling dropped him out of the top spot.

Even though none of his competitors were undefeated on the season, Anthony fell to the 7-seed. Many of the other coaches grumbled about the rule giving losses to wrestlers with less than fifteen matches because they knew that the 160 pound weight class would be the toughest one, as a 7-seed was the three-time defending regional champion, and the returning state runner-up. However, nothing could be done about it, as no exception was made for this type of a situation. Instead, everyone would have to be on top of their game as they'd surely be battle tested throughout the weekend.

Some coaches even considered bumping their wrestler to the 170 pound weight class to avoid the log jam of talent at 160. But, in the end, the wrestlers seeded above Anthony remained in place, leaving this to be the most watched weight class in the tournament, and would likely give the champion the Most Outstanding Wrestler Award. The remainder of the meeting went without a hitch and the Parkside coaching staff drove home happy and excited for the tournament to begin in two days.

After returning home, Vincent spent most of the event looking at the matchups and anticipating what would be needed for his entire team to place in the top four at regionals, and in-turn qualify for the state championships. Anthony joined in as Vincent played out a variety of scenarios and looked through all of his scouting reports on his athletes' opponents.

Anthony had slowly made his way back to studying film with Vincent and looking at ways to make the Mustangs better. And tonight, he sat up talking to Vincent for hours. It felt good to both of them, as a sense of normalcy had returned to their relationship. Anthony was no longer the angry, bitter, and hateful young man who was mourning the loss of his parents. Instead, he was once again, the determined athlete who was trying to win for more than just himself.

Anthony added to some of the scouting reports that Vincent had put together for the team as he had inside information that Vincent didn't possess because of how personable he was at tournaments. Enough so that athletes from other teams would do anything they could to have a conversation with him, which included his opponents or teammates of guys that would be wrestling one of the Mustangs that day. Undoubtedly, Anthony would come away with some type of a scouting report on the guys that his team would be facing. He'd find out about injuries or weaknesses that their opponents had, which gave his teammates a distinct advantage.

Vincent laughed at the notion that a teammate would give such information to an opponent, but he knew that Anthony was always talked about as being Mr. Congeniality. He was one of the most popular and well-known wrestlers in the area, which at times, he used for his teams benefit. And tonight, it was paying dividends for their preparation.

Friday and Saturday: February 13-14, 2015

The first day of the West Regional Championships had finally arrived. Throughout the half day, that the team was required to be in school, each wrestler checked their weight to make sure that there wouldn't be any problems later that afternoon. Coach Tanzino knew that not every scale was the same, so he had a philosophy that if his wrestlers were a half pound under on his scale, they should make weight on any scale out there. To Vincent, it was a precautionary measure to make sure everyone was on weight or below. Besides, if they were under on the first day, then it just gave them a little extra leeway for when they had to make weight the following morning.

The team left Parkside at 11:30am to make the hour and a half drive to check in at the hotel prior to making it to Saint Joe's as weigh-ins were being held at 3 and wrestling would begin at 4. Vincent was pleased to see that his team had properly controlled their weight throughout the week as there were no issues. Everyone was under-weight, enough so that their weigh-in the following day wouldn't be an issue.

Once weigh-ins finished, the Parkside Mustangs ate some food and rehydrated, as they got dressed in their singlets and warm-ups prior to their team meeting. It was one last time for Coach Tanzino to speak to all of them at once, since individual tournaments left each wrestler responsible for making sure that they were at the proper mat at the appropriate time with one of the coaches in their corner.

In their pre-tournament organization, the Mustangs found a corner of the gym to set up for the weekend. A place where they could go to in-between matches as well as where their friends and family could sit amongst the athletes as they cheered on the team.

Once everyone was there and focused on Coach Tanzino, Vincent spoke, "Okay guys, it's time for each of you to accomplish the goals that you set for yourself on the season. Many of you not only wanted to qualify for regionals, but place in the top four."

The entire team was focused as they wanted to make sure to obtain any morsel of knowledge that Vincent could offer prior to them stepping on the mat for what was inevitably going to be a significant challenge.

Vincent continued, "Each of you are responsible for your own diet throughout the day and to make sure you warm-up early enough that you have a good sweat going prior to stepping onto the mat for your match. Make sure you listen for your name to be called and to find a coach to be with you mat-side for your match. Remember; don't begin wrestling without one of the coaches sitting in the chair ready to help guide you when you need assistance. Do you all understand?"

Each of the wrestlers nodded their heads as they knew the importance of what he was asking of them. But none of this was new to the team, as they'd been through this on numerous occasions throughout the season. Yet, Vincent wanted to reiterate his points to make his expectations clear and to remind them that they've all been here before. Even though it was the regional championships, the team had been through similar situations for the past few months, so this wasn't anything new.

Vincent added, "Now, it's time for all of you to focus on the challenge in front of you. Each of you has your destiny in your hands. We as coaches can only inform you of ways to win, you need to execute them. I believe we're the most dominant team here and I know that all of you have what it takes to be successful this weekend. But having me believe it and you believe it are two different things. Remember, if you step on that mat and think you'll lose, you most likely will. Make sure your mind doesn't prevent you from winning. Focus on what you do well and how you can use it to your advantage. Believe in yourself and know that you've trained hard enough to be successful."

As he looked around at his team, he added, "Any questions?"

Nobody said anything as they were all aware of what was at stake and ready to get things started. Vincent had the entire team stand up in a circle, and put their hands together as Coach Tanzino called out, "Mustangs on three: one, two, three!"

In unison the team yelled, "Mustangs!"

As the tournament commenced, Anthony had to challenge himself to dig deep as he'd made significant gains in his conditioning, but wasn't where he used to be. As his first match approached, Anthony felt good. He knew that it would be a good warm-up for him before the difficult road ahead was encountered. He won his first match 18-4, handily beating the 10-seed. Anthony could have pinned his opponent on several occasions, but Coach Tanzino told him that he needed as much mat time as possible. It was a risky move to make since Anthony's conditioning wasn't what it used to be, but Vincent wanted Anthony to push himself and work through what might be a difficult situation. Vincent knew that the more confidence Anthony felt about his current ability to push through the matches, the better off he'd be the following weekend at states. Anthony did as he was asked to do, and at the end of three periods he felt good about lasting the entire time as he didn't feel too out of shape in doing so.

After his first round victory, Anthony was set to face the second seeded wrestler in the quarterfinal round, and another rematch with Travis Brown from South Hill. Travis was a returning state qualifier and place winner and a very familiar foe. They had already met twice during the season in the dual meet and at the Mid-West Conference Tournament finals, where Anthony earned two hard fought victories.

The quarterfinal match went back and forth, having each wrestler take an advantage, but when the clock struck zero at the end of the third, the score read 4-4, making another overtime match between the two of them a necessity. The combatants were evenly matched as the overtime period began, but Anthony obviously wanted it more as he went on the offensive as soon as the whistle blew. Anthony took shot after shot, forcing his opponent to sprawl and keep stepping back.

After four straight attempts, Anthony faked a shot, causing Travis to sprawl, but Anthony wasn't below him to defend; instead, Anthony backed out enough to pound on Travis' head and spin behind, earning a takedown to win the overtime match 6-4. As Anthony had his hand raised, he was pleased with his performance and that he had advanced to the semifinals and was halfway to achieving his goal for the weekend.

As Friday came to a close, the Mustangs had an enormous lead in the team standings as all fourteen athletes had made it to the second day. Only five of the wrestlers had even lost one match, but had won their other one to remain in the double elimination tournament. This left nine Mustangs in the championship bracket as they had reached the semi-finals, which was even more than Vincent could have asked for, but he was aware that the real challenge was still to come.

Saturday morning went off without a hitch as everyone made weight and was ready for what obstacle was ahead of them. The first round of the day was in the consolation bracket, before the semifinals would kick off. Parkside was poised to blow the tournament wide open as each member of the team was determined to place in the top four of their respective weight classes and qualify for the state championships.

As the tournament progressed to the 160 pound semifinal, Anthony found himself to be in a hostile environment. The semi-final round pitted Anthony against Zach Monroe from St. Joe's, the host school, and the number three seed. Zach had the distinct advantage of being at home, but Anthony didn't mind being in enemy territory as he'd been in this situation many times before. This would be another difficult match, but Anthony was prepared and determined to win.

Anthony fought throughout the back and forth battle against this formidable opponent. As he entered the third period, he had a slim 3-2 lead. Zach chose bottom, leaving Anthony to be placed on the top position to start the period. If Zach were to earn an escape, he'd tie the match, but if he were to earn a reverse, then Anthony would be losing by one point.

Anthony heard Coach Tanzino yelling for him to ride his opponent out, which was a risky strategy, but one that both of them were confident would work. Vincent wanted Anthony to show that he was a dominant force on top and that if he tried; nobody could get out from the bottom position. Anthony listened and did as was asked of him. He continuously grinded his opponent to the mat, making Zach work the entire time towards getting back to his base instead of trying to get out.

As the third period continued, Anthony threw in legs and did what was needed to keep them locked in. Even though Anthony couldn't turn this tough wrestler, he was able to completely control him for the final two minutes. His dominance allowed Anthony to pull out a 3-2 victory and make it into the regional finals against the top seeded Joseph Addison, and an opportunity to become a rare four time regional champion.

With his semifinal victory, Anthony had automatically qualified for the state championships the following weekend. But that wasn't enough for him as he wanted to win to give him a better shot at the state title by being seeded opposite of Jamie Wright. Both Vincent and Anthony understood how the state championships were seeded, as it gave the four regional champions the top four seeds and then placed everyone else according to what place they finished at their respective championships.

All champions would find themselves facing an opponent who had placed fourth in their regional tournament. This would allow the regional champions to have an easier first match and would guarantee that they didn't take on another regional champion for at least two matches. This gave a distinct edge to the wrestlers who were able to become regional champions, over someone who was second place.

The finals match posed a real threat to Anthony achieving his goals, since his opponent, Joseph Addison, had a 36-2 record going into the weekend. Joseph dominated all of his opponents throughout the season but one, Jaime Wright, who was able to beat him on two separate occasions. Joseph was a fierce competitor who placed third in the state championships in 2014 after also having been the runner-up to Anthony at regionals. Joseph was obviously thinking about revenge as he knew that Anthony wasn't at the competitive level that he once was.

The match was a strategic battle of technique and strength. Neither athlete was able to take a clear cut advantage, as they went back and forth. Both wrestlers aimed to be mistake free, only taking chances when they felt that the time was right. But after three periods, the match was tied 1-1, as each had earned an escape, sending Anthony to his second overtime match of the tournament.

Neither wrestler earned any points throughout the first overtime period or the two subsequent ride-out periods, forcing this battle to move to the ultimate 30 second sudden death ride-out period. Anthony lost the coin toss, leaving the decision of top or bottom to Joseph, who chose down. Anthony had 30 seconds to either score points or to prevent Joseph from earning any.

Throughout the ride-out period, Joseph showed how well-conditioned he was as he kept in constant motion, making it difficult for Anthony to control the match or keep him down. Yet, every time Joseph seemed to get an advantage and an opportunity to escape, Anthony quickly recovered. Time wasn't on either athlete's side as the seconds quickly ticked away. Joseph attempted to pull out all of the stops, while Anthony tried to weather the storm. Anthony's main focus was to not give up any type of a point; no matter what his opponent did.

After a hard fought 30 seconds and a near escape by Joseph, Anthony held on to win the ride-out period and along with it the match; earning him a 2-1 victory and his fourth regional championship as well as one of the top four seeds at states. His excitement for his fourth and final trip to the state championships was seen by all in attendance. But he was a gracious champion as he showed Joseph the utmost respect.

The rest of the Parkside Mustangs had faired similarly throughout the weekend, having seven of them advance to the finals, while three others landed in the consolation finals. This gave Parkside 10 state qualifiers and a dominant performance in the tournament. No other team had even half as many finalists and state qualifiers. Their success allowed the Mustangs to run away with their first regional championship in school history, by over 50 points, and another major accomplishment achieved.

They had attained another one of Coach Tanzino's goals for the season; a season that saw them rack up championship after championship, with only one more to go. Everyone was pleased with what they'd been able to do throughout the weekend. Even the four wrestlers who didn't qualify for states had made it to the consolation semi-finals and were only one match away from qualifying themselves.

After battling his way back against the top three seeds in the toughest weight class, Anthony was rewarded with the West Regional Most Outstanding Wrestler Award. Anthony was well liked by many of the other coaches, which ultimately helped him earn such an honor. Besides the fact that he had grinded out a number of impressive wins. Anthony was pleased with his results and earning the award, but knew that he couldn't have done it without the help of Coach Tanzino and his teammates. As the team gathered after receiving the trophy as the 4A West Regional Champions, Anthony wanted everyone to know that his MOW trophy wouldn't stay with him.

As a way to show his gratitude and understanding of what had taken place over the past few months, Anthony wanted to talk to his teammates and coaches, "I want to thank everyone for putting in the hard work to be standing atop our region. We've earned our right to fight for a state championship next weekend and I couldn't have gotten to this point without all of you, and especially Coach, which is why I don't deserve to have this trophy. This is for you Coach." Anthony handed the trophy over to Vincent and gave him a big hug. The team clapped as they saw the return of the old Anthony Williams as they knew that Coach deserved that trophy as much as anyone else.

Vincent appeared chocked up at this gesture, "Thank you Anthony and thank you everyone for everything you've done. All I ask is that you enjoy this for one day and then come to practice on Monday focused on states. Ten of you have qualified for next week's tournament, but all of you have earned the right to travel with us. I'm extremely proud of what you've done for this program. Mustangs on three: one, two, three!"

"Mustangs!" could be heard echoing throughout the gym, as the team showed off just how excited they were. Each day brought new challenges, but they faced those tests head on and were reaping the rewards. Ten out of fourteen starters would be getting an opportunity, in only a few short days, to showcase their talents and hard work at the state championships. They were all extremely proud of what the team had accomplished throughout the season, but this was a time for the individual to shine, and a moment to fulfill their own fate.

But, as the team showed their jubilation for another championship, all Anthony could think about was how it was time for him to focus on his attempt at obtaining that allusive title; the title that had been his ultimate goal and dream for the past four seasons; a title that would make all of his hard work and dedication worthwhile; the title that would truly honor the memory of his parents.

Chapter Twenty Five

The Week of the State Championships

February 16-19, 2015

The Parkside wrestlers had returned home, for the first time in school history, as regional champions. They had done so by obliterating the competition, while having ten out of fourteen wrestlers qualify for states; which included four regional champions and the regional MOW.

After wrestling his way through the top three seeds, Anthony had earned some respect back from many of the college coaches and recruiters. He wasn't quite the same wrestler he'd been prior to his time off, but glimpses of greatness and confidence in his ability were carrying him a long way. Coach Tanzino warned Anthony that even though he was once again a regional champion and back at states, that things were different. They both realized that extra work was needed throughout the week leading up to his last chance at achieving the lone goal that had eluded him throughout his career.

Anthony was prepared to do whatever it took over the next few days. He even asked Vincent if they could get some extra workouts in before school and stay late to increase his stamina, along with working on moves that would help him defeat Jamie Wright, who he'd likely face in the finals if they both made it. Vincent agreed and invited the rest of the team to join them, which was well received. All ten state qualifiers made their way to school extra early each morning, to get a light workout in.

Coach Tanzino didn't want to over work his athletes, so he took the extra time to tweak a few mistakes that they'd made and gave each of them an opportunity to get a light lift in. Vincent had completed many similar workouts in his college career and knew some of the benefits of getting their bodies moving in the morning. It allowed each of his athletes to loosen up any sore muscles and gave them a slight edge over the tough competition that they'd be facing throughout the upcoming weekend.

As the week progressed, the excitement and the buzz filled the air of the halls of Parkside High School and in the practice facility. The team not only had individual dreams, but many of them realized that they could make a clean sweep of every title. They had already won every tournament that they'd entered throughout the regular season, the conference championship, a dual team championship, along with a regional championship, and now had their goals set on the team title for the 4A individual state championships.

Each wrestler set their personal goal for the weekend and pushed themselves accordingly. Vincent had everything running efficiently. Each athlete did whatever they deemed necessary to accomplish their goal, while Vincent sat back and gave them the freedom to do as little or as much as they needed throughout the week. Vincent wasn't surprised that the majority of the guys were working just as hard if not harder than they normally would. Everyone's weight seemed to be under control and they were taking great care of themselves. All of which made Vincent proud, as he'd finally achieved many of his own dreams and his athletes were doing what was required to achieve theirs.

The tournament was scheduled to begin on Friday morning, which allowed the team to train in their own facility until Thursday afternoon prior to heading to the hotel where they'd remain for two nights as they challenged the best wrestlers in the state.

The entire school was electric throughout the week. Each wrestler had been congratulated over and over again, but Vincent warned each of them that they shouldn't rest on just making it there, and that their work was incomplete. Vincent didn't want to see his wrestlers get swept up in the hype and the buzz that had surrounded them throughout the season and had tremendously grown over the past few weeks. The team did a great job of grounding themselves and making sure that they thanked everyone for supporting and believing in them, but deep down each wrestler knew that they had more work to do.

Thursday: February 19, 2015

As the team left Parkside High School Thursday evening after practice, it felt as though a caravan was following them to the hotel. Many of the parents had taken the opportunity to join the team on this trip and even some of the student body decided to miss school the following day to watch the team earn further personal accolades.

This brought added responsibility and pressure to Vincent, as he had to make sure that none of his athletes were bothered by their friends and family, but had the necessary rest and focus to accomplish their goals. This caused Vincent to set a curfew, not only for when each athlete would be in their room, but when he expected his athletes to go to bed along with when they could be on their cell phones.

Vincent made his rules clear to his athletes as well as every parent and Parkside student he came in contact with. He wanted all of his athletes to have every opportunity to do their best that weekend, without any distractions. Even though he was clear on his rules, Vincent heard some grumblings, not from his athletes or even their parents, but from his athletes girlfriends, who were not happy with the separation that Vincent was imposing on them.

The wrestlers didn't think twice about his requests and did as coach asked since they knew that he'd taken them this far, so why not listen and follow his explicit instructions. The team knew that Coach Tanzino was only looking out for their best interest, as he wanted nothing more than to see each wrestler achieve their goals. Everyone did what was expected of them and each knew in the long run, they'd be thankful for their results.

Unbeknownst to them, Vincent had been contacting college coaches throughout the week to make sure that they kept an eye on a few of his wrestlers who could easily earn themselves a scholarship with their performance. He wanted to make sure the coaches had representatives specifically watching his athletes, because he not only knew that they could be successful at the next level, but he also wanted to help provide each of them with an opportunity for a successful life beyond athletics.

Vincent believed that by helping his athletes earn scholarships, he was changing their lives for the better. Coach knew the importance of earning a college degree and he wanted to do everything in his power to help. Vincent felt strongly that his athletes deserved an opportunity to better themselves, and do so with the financial burden of paying for their tuition. He knew how tough it was to be successful in life and to make enough money to survive. Which is why he didn't want his athletes to struggle; instead, his desire was to give each of them a chance at a better life for themselves and the family that they may one day have.

The recruiting had thinned out for Anthony throughout his personal ordeal, as the number of teams that wanted him to be a part of their program on a scholarship had been cut in half, but Vincent had been diligent on working every connection he had. Vincent knew that when Anthony got past the difficult situation that he'd been through, he'd still want to compete in college, and do so on a scholarship. And now that his parents were gone, Vincent was even more cognizant of how much he'd have to help Anthony grow up into a well-rounded man. Fortunately for Vincent, Anthony was well on his way of becoming one before he even met him, but had grown even more since he joined the team.

Even though a number of teams had stopped recruiting Anthony, Vincent had been able to keep a few interested. Vincent made sure to contact the recruiters himself each step of the way while Anthony had been working his way back. Coach knew that whatever school ended up signing Anthony would be getting a dominant athlete that would do whatever it took to succeed on and off the wrestling mat; and an athlete that would stop at nothing to become a National Champion.

Chapter Twenty Six

2015 North Carolina State Championships

Friday and Saturday: February 20th-21st, 2015

The weekend of the 2015 North Carolina State Wrestling Championships had finally arrived and the Parkside Mustangs were in full force. The team had accomplished more than Vincent's wildest dreams could have imagined, but they weren't finished yet. It was now time for each wrestler to take their fate into their own hands. Vincent could only try to motivate and aid his athletes so much; it was their personal desires and drive that would provide each of them with whatever success they were bound for.

The team had high expectations as they clearly had the numbers to win the individual state tournament title, to go along with all of their other accolades throughout the season. They had the most state qualifiers in the 4A division, as the next closest team only had seven. This gave them an edge in the team race, but Vincent knew that it was still going to have to be won on the mat.

For half of The Parkside Mustangs, this was a new experience, as it was their first trip to states. They understood what it took for them to succeed, as they realized that they possessed the tools necessary to place in the top six in their respective weight classes. The next two days would push each of them to their limits, but every member of the team knew that they'd put in enough hard work and had dedicated adequate time towards achieving their goals. No one understood this more than Anthony, as he was making his fourth attempt at becoming a state champion; the only trophy that was missing from his collection.

Anthony was given the overall number three seed for the 160 pound weight class, while his arch nemesis Jamie Wright was the one seed. This put the two of them on a crash course to meet each other in the final match of the tournament; if they were both able to make it there. Anthony's first two matches were easier than he would've expected, as he won 12-1 and 9-2 respectively, landing him in the semifinal match against the number 2-seed and another regional champion.

This appeared to be a tough match, but by this point it was expected that any match would be difficult. His opponent, David Henderson, who hailed from the Raleigh area, was talented, but didn't end up posing as much of a threat as most of the matches Anthony faced the previous weekend. Anthony had either lucked out and found an easier path throughout the tournament or all of the extra work that he'd put in was paying off. Anthony wrestled a technically sound semifinal as he controlled every aspect of the six minute match. His dominance was impressive as he was never in jeopardy of losing. Anthony was able to bring home the victory with a 7-2 score; earning himself a spot in the finals, and once again, against Jamie Wright, the reigning state champion.

However, Jamie's path was paved with complete and utter dominance. None of his opponents lasted beyond the second period as he won his first match 16-0, his second match 17-2 against Travis Brown, and he pinned his semifinal opponent, Joseph Addison, in 2:52. Jamie wanted to send a message to Anthony that he could destroy two common opponents in a manner that Anthony wasn't able to. Jamie had put himself in a position to become a two-time state champion and the tournament MOW for a second straight season. The only thing standing in his way was a rematch against Anthony Williams, an opponent who had battled through adversity to even make it to this point.

Anthony wasn't the only Mustang to take advantage of this opportunity. They saw a tremendous amount of success as seven out of the ten wrestlers put themselves in position to finish in the top six, while every one of the athletes won at least one match. Throughout the championship match-ups, the Mustangs saw Ryan Thompson finish in third place at heavyweight, Matt States finish fourth at 106, Mike Robinson finish fifth at 220, while Tyron Johnson finished in sixth place at 145.

The success that they achieved made them the front runners to win the team title. The only way they could lose was if all three of their finalists were defeated and the second place team earned pins in all of their finals matches; but one win by the Mustangs would guarantee another championship. The 170 pound final pitted opponents from each of the top two teams, leaving that as a possible winner take all match-up, if it even got to that point.

However, Chris and Anthony had an opportunity to solidify the championship even before Tim had a chance to step on the mat for his match. Chris' finals match didn't go as expected as he uncharacteristically made a mistake allowing his opponent to take Chris down to his back and quickly earn five points, which put Chris behind, enough so that he was never able to fully recover.

Chris gave everything he had to claw his way back, but his opponent never had to open up as he became a defensive wrestler for the remainder of the match. At the end, even though Chris wasn't victorious, a second place finish was quite an accomplishment, putting a smile on Chris' face as he walked to the edge of the mat and hugged Coach Tanzino. He hadn't achieved his final goal, but he was still proud of himself and everything that he'd helped his team achieve.

Much like the previous years' championship round, the roar of the crowd could be heard downstairs while Anthony and Tim warmed up. Anthony and Tim took turns taking shots and finishing them, before working on defenses to takedowns that their opponents regularly used. Afterwards, they proceeded to work on top and bottom moves. Anthony worked at breaking Tim down three times along with working his tilts or various other pinning combinations, before Tim would do the same. Then each of them worked on bottom, where they tried to stop breakdowns and near fall attempts that they might see from their opponent.

Once both of them had a good sweat going, they stretched some more and then moved around on their own, just enough to keep warm and get mentally prepared. Anthony took that time alone to focus on what was ahead of him. He played the match over and over again in his mind. He knew what moves would work and what to watch for.

This also gave him time to think about his parents. Anthony thought about last years' finals, and the last night that he saw them alive, before thinking about how things would be different if they were there in the stands. Anthony was sad that they weren't physically there, but he was resolved to believe that they were watching from above.

Just a few minutes before he was called to enter the arena floor, Vincent approached Anthony. As Vincent reached him, Anthony spoke, "Wow, this seems eerily familiar, like I've been here before."

"You've been in this position many times in your career. Just remember, it's just another match," stated Vincent as he was worried that Anthony was putting too much pressure on himself.

"Yeah, another match for a North Carolina State Championship!" exclaimed Anthony.

"Yes, it's for a state championship, but don't think about that. You've trained to be successful in every match that you've wrestled, this is no different. It's amazing how you made it back here after everything you went through. Win or lose, I'm proud to be your coach and I know your parents are proud of you as well."

Anthony sadly added, "I just wish they were here to watch me wrestle this match."

Vincent reassured Anthony, "They are. As long as they remain in your heart and in your mind, they'll always be with you no matter what you're doing."

"I know T. I'm thankful for everything they've done for me and what you have as well. I put you through hell and I'm sorry for it."

"I understand. You've gone through a difficult time and I'm glad I was able to help. Just know, I love you like you're family and I'd do anything I can for you."

Anthony and Vincent embraced, which was exactly what Anthony needed. As they hugged, Anthony told Vincent just how much he loved him. They'd been through so much together, and today was just another chapter in their book. Win or lose, Vincent would be just as proud of Anthony.

Once the embrace was over, they headed out of the warm-up area and made their way to the hallway that led into the arena floor. They were both excited as it was almost time for the match to be underway.

When Anthony's name was called, they were escorted by one of the event staff members until they arrived at the center mat, where most of the crowd's attention was already focused.

As they made their way to the mat, the announcer began introducing both wrestlers to the crowd. "The 160 pound championship bout is a rematch of last years' thrilling 152 pound final. Anthony Williams came in regarded as the best wrestler in the state last year and lost during the final seconds. During the off-season, he went on to win three high school national championships.

"On the other side, after winning the title, Jamie has continued right where he left off as he's on an 85 match regular season winning streak coming into tonight. Jamie has to be the favorite in this match as Anthony missed half of the season due to a tragic event in his life. His parents died in a car accident in November and it wasn't until the middle of January that Anthony returned to the mat. Due to the loss of his parents, Anthony was placed in the care of his Head Coach, Vincent Tanzino, the highly regarded coach who's done a marvelous job building up his program into the dual team state champions.

"Many people believed that the time off of the mat would have prevented Anthony from making it this far; however, Anthony gutted out a number of wins to make it back to the finals. It's a feel good story to see Anthony Williams on the mat as he's come back from adversity, but it's hard to believe that he'll be able to pull out this win as Jamie's been on the top of his game all season long. Jamie has already signed a letter of intent to wrestle collegiately at the University of North Carolina at Chapel Hill and hasn't had any opponent even come close to defeating him this year. The rolls have truly reversed as we have what should be the most exciting match of the evening."

While the announcer continued to discuss the upcoming bout, Anthony stripped down to his singlet, placed his headgear on his head and gave Coach Tanzino one last hug before checking into the table. Jamie was already at the center of the mat waiting for his opponent and for the rematch that he was clearly favored in this time around.

Jamie had an air of confidence around him, which some might have even called arrogance. He knew that he'd beaten Anthony once before and had been training all year long for this opportunity, while Anthony's extended time away from the sport had caused him to lose a step or two. Jamie was confident that if he continued to press the pace of the match that Anthony couldn't keep up with him.

After checking in, Anthony made his way to the center of the mat. He grabbed the green ankle band to place it on his right ankle. While Anthony was down on one knee placing the band around his ankle, he said one final prayer to his parents and thanked them for watching over him and giving him the strength to win the only championship that had eluded him.

Once Anthony stood up and placed his right foot on the line, the official prompted both athletes to shake hands. After they complied, the referee blew his whistle, signifying the beginning of the match. Jamie wasted no time as he swiftly began to attack. He pressed forward, pushing Anthony backwards as he began to work his set-ups. Anthony was surprised at how aggressive Jamie was, since it was he who had pressed the action throughout the match just a year earlier. But, before Anthony knew what happened, Jamie had used inside control to hit a duck under and a quick two points for the takedown.

Anthony made a number of valiant attempts to move from the bottom, but Jamie had a tight grip on him, preventing Anthony from going anywhere. Jamie used his positioning to hit a quick tilt, which he was only able to hold for two seconds, earning him two near fall points and a 4-0 lead with over a minute still remaining in the first period. Anthony was exerting a tremendous amount of energy as he continued to work to get to his feet. He was finally able to clear some space between him and Jamie in order to hit a hard stand up. But as soon as he earned the one point escape, Jamie was already in on a double leg takedown to earn an additional two points, giving him a 6-1 lead as the time ran out of the first period.

The feeling of the match was very different than the previous one. Jamie was dominating the pace and the action, while Anthony seemed to be on his heels causing him to be indecisive. Anthony glanced at Coach Tanzino, looking for some words of wisdom from a man that was his mentor, friend, and now his guardian. Vincent yelled, "Anthony, everything's okay. Calm down and work your moves. You can do this, I believe in you."

Anthony looked back to the center of the mat, and saw the official flip his coin, which landed on red, meaning Jamie had the choice for the second period or he could defer it so that he had it during the third period. Instead of deferring his choice to the third period, Jamie picked bottom and immediately got set on the mat, as he felt that this was the best way to add to his lead.

Jamie looked confident and at ease with this match, while Anthony seemed a little uptight. Once the official saw that both competitors were set, he blew his whistle. Jamie moved quickly, while Anthony looked as if he was a second too slow. Jamie hit a stand up and immediately began attacking Anthony. They both tried to set up their moves, but once again, Jamie was successful. This time hitting a fireman's carry, putting Anthony right on his back for a five second count and an additional three points before Anthony maneuvered his body out of bounds.

Jamie now had a commanding 12-1 lead with more than half of the second period remaining. As the action started back up, both wrestlers attempted to gain an advantage, yet neither of them were successful. With fifteen seconds left and down by eleven points, Anthony felt a burst of energy. Anthony gave everything he had and continuously moved his body to create enough space for himself to sit out and hit a switch. This earned him two points for the reversal, cutting the lead to 12-3 as the period ended.

Anthony stood up, looked at the scoreboard, and saw that he was down by nine points with only two minutes left. He glanced over to Coach Tanzino, as it was his choice for the third period.

Coach Tanzino encouraged Anthony as he shouted, "Take a deep breath. Look at what you just did at the end of the period. See, you can do this. You can win this match. Two more minutes until glory."

Anthony nodded his head as if he knew Coach was right and that he wasn't out of this match yet. He hadn't come back after everything that had happened to him just to lose. The score didn't indicate it, but deep down, he knew that it was his match for the taking. It had to be, as it was the best way that he could honor his parents.

Vincent called out instructions as Anthony got ready for the start of the third period, "We need as many points as we can get, you need to go down and explode just like you did at the end of the second. Just keep scoring points. And remember, he's beatable. You can do this, if not for me or yourself, do this for your parents."

That's all Anthony needed to hear. All of a sudden his demeanor changed and he looked like a man resolved to succeed at all costs. He quickly got himself set on the mat, before Jamie got on top. Anthony anticipated the officials whistle and exploded at the exact instant that the referee signified the beginning of the period. The explosion gave him plenty of space to turn into Jamie, gaining his one point escape and great position on the inside. Jamie was still reacting to the escape when Anthony took a high crotch shot right into a double leg finish.

Before he knew what hit him, Jamie had already given up three points, and only ten seconds had run off of the clock. Anthony continued to react faster than Jamie could as he threw legs in and begin to control his hips. Anthony hit a Jacob's hook and waiting to see the referee finish his five count; earning another three points. He was now only down by three, as the state championship was within his grasp.

Anthony saw that the tides had turned and that there was still hope for him. He had been filled with an unusual amount of energy and a peculiar inner peace. Everything seemed to be in slow motion as he anticipated Jamie's every move, completely frustrating his opponent. The only explanation he could come up with was that his parents were helping him through this difficult situation, like guardian angels.

The seconds continued to tick away, forcing Anthony to be mindful of how much time was left. They had to figure out a strategy and quickly as there was only 45 seconds remaining and he was still down by three. Should Anthony let him up and take him down, cutting into the lead, or try to turn him. But the decision was being made for him as he clearly heard Coach Tanzino yelling for him to turn Jamie and finish him off. It was a gutsy move, but Anthony knew that it was the right move as Coach had never led him astray.

Jamie maneuvered himself in a position that he was able to free himself of the clutches of Anthony's legs and squirted his way out of bounds to get a fresh start. Now, with only 20 seconds left, Anthony knew that this was his moment to make his move. As soon as they were set and the whistle blew, Anthony chopped Jamie's left arm and tied it up with his right hand. Anthony jammed his left hand through the hole between Jamie's arm and body in order to obtain a bar arm position. Anthony used his right leg to block Jamie's left leg, using the fact that Jamie couldn't post that left arm out to prevent Anthony from running the move.

Anthony settled in and turned Jamie right to his back. The official began to count as the seconds ran off of the clock. Anthony knew that if he couldn't pin him, then he'd have at least tied up the score, forcing overtime. But overtime wasn't needed, as the official blew the whistle and slapped the mat with only five seconds left on the clock. Anthony had earned the pin and the win, bringing with it a state championship not only for himself, but for the Parkside Mustangs as well. Anthony had finally won the only title that had eluded him, a North Carolina Individual State Championship.

Anthony stood up, unhooked his headgear and pulled it off of his head. As the referee had Anthony and Jamie shake hands, the smile on Anthony's face grew wider and the tears began to stream down his face. The official raised Anthony's hand, and turned the champion around, showing the capacity crowd of 15,000 spectators that he was the North Carolina 160 pound state champion.

Once the official let go of Anthony's left arm, he reached into his headgear and pulled out an item that he'd placed in there the day that he returned to wrestling, a picture of his parents. He kissed the picture and then raised it up to the sky, placing one finger up in the air, indicating his first place finish, while mouthing to the heavens, "I love you," as tears trickled down his face.

As Anthony turned towards Coach Tanzino, the tears continued to flow. Anthony walked up to Vincent and gave him a huge hug. They embraced, letting everyone in the arena see the emotions ooze out of them. The embrace lasted for what felt like an eternity to both of them and was exactly what they needed.

As he held on tight, Anthony spoke, "Thank you Coach for believing in me and helping me through it all. This championship is as much yours as it is mine or my parents. I love you."

"I'm honored to be your coach and to call you and your parents' family. I'm so proud of you and I know your parents are in Heaven smiling down on you right now."

The two of them remained in the corner of the mat, with one arm around each other, tears in their eyes and smiles on their faces. They both finally accomplished what they'd worked so hard for. But neither had much time to focus on it, as Tim was up next. Vincent wiped away his tears as Tim approached the center mat. Tim didn't need a big pep talk as he was already focused on what he needed to do. Vincent sat at the edge of the mat, with Anthony behind him, as he watched another one of his athletes accomplish greatness.

Tim followed suit as he dominated his opponent, earning a pin in the second period, and with it, the 170 pound state championship. This gave Vincent two state champions to go along with sweeping the team championships throughout the season. Anthony was awarded the tournament MOW Award as he got revenge for his lone loss over the past two years, while making a tremendous comeback on the season and in his final match. Anthony deservedly so, finally accomplished what he'd set out to do; and in doing so, honored his parents. In-spite of their physical absence, Anthony felt close to them as his love for them filled his heart and put a smile on his face. His dreams had come true and he had his parents to thank for it.

Chapter Twenty Seven

The Parkside Cemetery

Sunday: March 1st, 2015

It was a beautiful sunny afternoon, as Vincent drove Anthony to the Parkside Cemetery. It felt like spring was in the air on such a gorgeous day. Anthony could have driven himself, but he wanted Coach to be there with him. Anthony needed some time alone with his parents, but he wanted to feel the strength and support that Coach Tanzino had always given him, even throughout his darkest hours.

As Vincent parked his Jeep, he remained seated, allowing Anthony some alone time with his parents. Anthony slowly walked down the row of headstones until he came upon the one that meant so much to him, his parents. Anthony stood there, staring at the names on the stone. He read the inscription, which brought tears to his eyes. His parents meant so much to him as they'd been there for him throughout all of his failures and even more successes.

They'd supported him in every way, while giving him every opportunity to make something of his life and he was grateful for it. But now their physical bodies were gone as they were resolved to watch him from Heaven. It took him some time to work past what happened and realize that even though they weren't physically there, that they'd always be in his mind and his heart. Their distance wasn't going to keep them from having a relationship. It was only going to change it and give Anthony something to look forward to many years down the road when he was reunited with them.

Anthony hadn't gone empty handed to the grave as he was carrying a few items that he wanted to share with his parents. He showed his parents the picture that he had of them in his headgear and the medal that he had received just a few days earlier. He also was holding onto a letter.

As Anthony stood there with these items, he began to talk to them, "Mom, Dad, I did it! I beat Jamie and won a state championship. I've finished what we set out to accomplish. I just wanted to thank you for everything that you've done for me. I know that you guys made a lot of sacrifices to provide for me and I truly appreciate it. You'll be glad to hear that I've got my grades back on track and that I'll be graduating.

"I also earned a full ride to West Virginia University and it's all because Coach always believed in me. He used his connections to keep them interested while I was grieving. Thanks for trusting him to guide me throughout the rest of my life as he's taking great care of me. He's learning, but he'll have more help soon. Coach asked Vanessa to marry him and she said 'Yes!' They even want me to be the Best Man, so that a piece of you guys are able to be in the wedding. Just know that I'll always have you in my heart as I know that you'll be watching over me from above. I miss you guys so much and I love both of you with all my heart!"

A moment later, Anthony set his scholarship letter down in the flower pot that sat next to his parents' headstone. He then placed the picture and the medal on the bottom of the headstone. He wanted his parents to have them, because without them, he wouldn't have had the opportunity to be where he was at, or even to continue his dream at the collegiate level. Anthony knelt down next to the grave, and kissed each of his parents' names. He stood up with tear filled eyes as he took one last look before walking back towards Coach Tanzino, who was now standing outside of his vehicle.

Anthony approached Vincent and immediately gave him a hug. Anthony held on tight and let out some of the tears and emotions that had built up over the past four months. Vincent embraced Anthony for as long as he needed. Anthony let the tears fall from his eyes, releasing the anguish that he felt. He had a fresh start to his life and he was grateful for it. Once Anthony was done releasing his emotions, he thanked Coach Tanzino for all that he'd done for him throughout the years and was glad that he'd remain in his life, not as a father, but as a best friend or like an older brother.

Anthony slowly let go of Vincent, walked to his side of the vehicle, opened the door, and got in. He took one more look back at his parents' grave and smiled at them as Vincent drove off.

CPSIA information can be obtained
at www.ICGtesting.com
Printed in the USA
FFOW04n1849020816
26423FF